STEP-BY-STEP SEO

The Complete Guide To Search Engine Success

MATTHEW DAVIDSON

ISBN: 061567660X

ISBN 13: 9780615676609

Table of Contents

Foreword

As you read this book and come to understand the specific activities required to take the success of your website into your own hands, I strongly encourage you to visit me at **www.stepbystepseobook.com** and sign up for my monthly newsletter. At various times while you work on your search engine presence, I will provide you with additional tips, tricks, resources, and the occasional discount for top-rated SEO tools, which will help you expedite your search engine efforts and, as a result, online success.

Why I Wrote This Book

I have worked in search engine marketing for over a decade. In that time, I've attended dozens of conferences, worked with hundreds of advertisers, and read thousands of articles on the topic of search engine optimization. After learning about the potential impact search engine optimization can have on business success, I made it my personal goal to learn how to effectively optimize websites for strong search engine placement.

However, as I set about learning the process of getting to that magical position at the top of the search engines, I was frustrated at the lack of specific information available on how I could improve my search engine visibility. There were a lot of buzzwords and tips, but nothing I found useful for applying specific strategies to my everyday efforts. Thus, after years of trial and error, I decided to write a book providing the exact process and resources utilized by professionals such as myself. With this book, now anyone can succeed with search engine optimization and enjoy increased online traffic and visibility as a result.

Introduction

Step-by-Step SEO Method

The goal with the Step-by-Step SEO Method is to provide you with a concrete plan, things you can do today to begin increasing your search engine rankings and improving your online business. Rather than present a bunch of high-level recommendations, this book is designed to provide you with an easy-to-follow action plan that you can implement to start increasing your search engine rankings immediately.

How This Book Is Organized

This book is structured to provide you with a breakdown of each strategy and how to apply it to your own search engine optimization efforts. Each chapter provides detailed recommendations for tools, resources, and processes to complete these tasks. At the end of the book, there is a specific action plan you may reference weekly as you continue to work on your search engine optimization program. I strongly encourage you to read the entire book first and then go back and implement each area outlined.

After reading *Step-by-Step SEO*, you will be well on your way to becoming a knowledgeable search engine marketer who can tremendously impact the amount of traffic and business you are able to drive online.

I hope you enjoy reading this book as much as I have enjoyed writing it.

Chapter 1

Why Search Engines Matter and What to Do About It

Did you know that over 90 percent of the adult population uses a search engine? Were you aware that, other than e-mail, search is the most popular online activity? Did you have any idea that Google processes over *two billion* searches every single day? With statistics as staggering as these, is it any wonder that search engine optimization has become a major component of improving online visibility? With this book, my goal is to help you understand how search engines work and how your website can become more relevant in their eyes.

So what exactly is search engine optimization (SEO) and why is it so important to anyone looking to attract online business? SEO is important because search is important.

Consumers are changing and so are their preferences for how they want to engage with business. Potential customers are overwhelmed with advertising coming at them from all directions, such as billboards, radio, television, direct mail, telemarketing, and more. This overabundance has resulted in a lower tolerance for intrusive advertising.

That is why search engine optimization has become such a necessity in modern-day advertising. Instead of shouting your message at your prospective customers, you can sit back and let your customers find you at the exact moment they are looking for what you have to offer.

This could very well be the reason that sales leads coming through SEO average a closing rate of 14.6 percent while outbound leads (such as print advertising or direct mail) average a closing rate of only 1.7 percent, according to a study conducted by *Search Engine Journal* (a respected resource on advertising). This same study found that 40 percent of SEO marketers interviewed experienced a return on their investment in excess of 500 percent. Just take a second to think about how powerful those kinds of advertising returns could be for any business.

Search engine optimization is all about traffic and location. If you own a restaurant, you will find it most profitable to build your restaurant in a busy area with bustling foot traffic. Similarly, the most profitable websites appear at or near the top of everyday popular searches within the most active and biggest search engines. Getting to the top of the search engines is important. Websites that use search engine optimization to target their audience have repeat visitors, often get shared socially, and are more likely to convert new customers online.

Over the past decade, I have lived, breathed, and slept search engine marketing, for I'm a believer. I've visited Google's ridiculously extravagant headquarters. I spent four years working at Microsoft on its Bing.com search engine. For the past three years, I have been running an SEO agency whose sole focus is to get websites to that enviable position at the top of the search engines.

I have personally witnessed countless situations in which high search engine rankings have produced significant increases in business, phone calls, sales, and overall brand awareness. I've been fortunate to work with hundreds of individuals, businesses, and organizations that have used search engine optimization on their websites to achieve incredible success.

During my time working directly for a search engine, and later with my own agency, I've assisted hundreds of businesses in building their client base through search engine exposure. I worked with a roofing company in Seattle that wanted to increase calls and land more jobs during the rare months in Seattle when it isn't raining. I worked with a community bank in Montana that needed to build brand awareness and open more checking and savings accounts. I even worked with an Alaskan preservation group determined to help protect and restore the wild salmon and trout population throughout the state—a worthy cause, to be sure. You know what they all had in common? In each case, these entities applied the strategies outlined in this book to reach their objectives. Although their aims and objectives were very different, the outcomes were all the same: overwhelming success in reaching their online goals.

These are just some of the many cases I've witnessed where improving search engine traffic has made the difference between a good attempt and a successful venture. Whether you're establishing a new business, developing an existing one, or simply trying to build awareness for a website or cause important to you, working with the search engines to improve your online visibility could absolutely be the determining factor of your success.

Allow me to formally introduce myself. In 2006, Microsoft launched adCenter, and I was recruited to help advertisers market themselves through this new paid search platform. Over the next four years, I experienced an evolution of smarter search engine marketing, the launch of Bing.com, and an integration between Microsoft and Yahoo! to increase search engine dominance.

At the beginning of the Yahoo! integration, I left Microsoft to start my own search engine agency. At Sovo Media, my primary focus has been working with business owners to meet their online goals, and as such, I've been exposed to hundreds of opportunities to drive increased search engine rankings. While the only guarantees in life are death and taxes, and it is true that even the best SEO professionals aren't successful 100 percent of the time, I will say that I have had a consistent track record of success. In this book, I'll reveal the exact process, techniques, and tools I use to achieve these types of results.

My intent with this book is to give you the tools and resources you need to apply these same techniques and to experience similar success. What can you expect by increasing your search engine rankings? Success on the search engines typically leads to increased web traffic and visibility, a spike in interested visitors to your website, and the resulting benefit of more awareness, phone calls, and online sales through your web presence.

Before we get started, I would like to introduce a quick history lesson. In 1996, two Stanford classmates had a vision to organize all of the information found on the web in a relevant and manageable way. To say that this was a challenging task is an understatement. Billions of web pages with information on every imaginable topic can be found on the Internet today. And the place most people now visit when searching for information? Google—the brainchild of those two Stanford classmates.

Throughout this book, I'll discuss the strategies I use to get websites ranked on search engines like Google for the search terms most relevant for their products and services. Within this book, I primarily refer to strategies geared toward positively impacting Google searches, since Google currently accounts for around 70 percent of all search engine traffic. Plus, when you optimize for Google, you will typically experience increases on the rest of the search engines as well.

As a reference, here is a current breakdown of search engine traffic by individual search engine:

Search Engine Market Share Report

Search Engine	Search Share (%)
Google	67.0%
Microsoft	16.2%
Yahoo!	12.1%
Ask Network	3.0%
AOL	1.7%

Source: comScore - a global leader in measuring the digital world and marketing intelligence.

While I often refer to Google, please note that these tactics will typically assist with increased exposure across all of the search engines. However, it's much easier to focus your attention specifically on Google given the search market share it currently enjoys.

My goal with this book isn't to help you beat the system. In fact, it's the opposite. I want to help you figure out the best way to make the search engines understand what your site is about and why they should give you priority for the search terms you deem important. By working with the search engines, you can drive significantly more traffic to your website and create a better experience for the searcher as well. It's a win-win situation: the search engines provide better information to their users, while you get more traffic to your site. And when everybody wins, it's a good day!

Search engine optimization has acquired a negative perception over the years. Some people see SEO as trying to trick and manipulate the search engines into giving their sites preferential treatment. I'll let you in on a secret. The search engines *want* you to do optimization—because it makes their searches better. A search engine's business is built on offering searchers relevant information. When you make *your* information more relevant to searchers, the search engines benefit and, more importantly, so do you.

Let's begin with why search engines matter. As mentioned earlier, over 90 percent of the adult population uses search engines to find information. It seems that Internet users have become preconditioned to go to a search engine first. Many have set a search engine as their default home page. In fact, many Internet users will go to a search engine to find a site even when they already know the name of the site they're trying to locate!

Take a look at this recent data from the Pew Research Center:

	% of each group who ever use search engines	% of each group who uses search engines on a typical day
All online adults	92%	59%
Gender		
Male	93	61
Female	91	57
Race/Ethnicity		
White	93	60
African American	91	57
Hispanic	87	48
Age		
18-29	96	66
30-49	91	64
50-64	91	52
65+	87	37
Education		
Some high school	81	29
High school	88	41
Some college	94	66
College graduate	96	75
Household income		
< $30,000	90	38
$30,000 - $49,999	91	67
$50,000 - $74,999	93	66
$75,000+	98	78

Source: The Pew Research Center's Internet & American Life Project, April 26 – May 22, 2011 tracking survey.

As you can see, getting ranked on search engines has become something of a necessity. By getting ranked, I'm referring to the process of having your website show up on the search engines for search terms relevant to your site.

Unfortunately, how to get ranked has proven extremely confusing for many website owners. But it doesn't have to be some unknown black hole. Careful consideration goes into Google's search engine placement, and discovering how those decisions are made can make all the difference.

Search engines are continuously crawling the web while seeking out new pages and content. They aren't overly sophisticated, as they can read text and links but not much else. When you conduct a search, the results are displayed almost magically, but a lot is happening behind the scenes. In this book, I'll uncover these mysteries so that anyone who wants to be found on Google will have an opportunity to do so.

When I started my agency, I did extensive research, went to conferences, made friends with other search engine marketing firms, and spent a tremendous amount of time and money to truly understand how and what it means to rank highly on the search engines.

What I share in this book isn't some random theory about why search engines give preference to some websites over others. It isn't meant to be a general outline of what to look out for. It was born out of real-world results and is designed to be a concise, easy-to-implement process that, if followed diligently, should help you garner better results on the search engines. Again, as a word of caution, nothing is ever guaranteed in the world of search engine optimization, as any SEO professional can attest. That being said, you really have nothing to lose by implementing the strategies outlined in this book.

Chapter 2

Not All Search Terms Are Created Equal

When selecting which search terms, also known as keywords, you want to rank highly for, there are three important factors to consider: which keywords are most relevant for your site, which keywords have low competition, and which keywords have high search volume.

Formula for keyword research:

Low Competition
+
High Search Volume
+
High Visitor Value
=
Reaching Searchers Successfully

To discern which keywords make the most sense to optimize for your site, here is a 4-step process to identify the best keywords to target with your SEO efforts.

Step 1) Put together a list of keywords you think someone would use to find you.

Step 2) Go to the Google Keyword Tool here: **https://adwords.google.com/o/KeywordTool** and type in the list of keywords you came up with. Then once you've entered the target search terms, click on the search button to reveal a list of related terms and their corresponding monthly traffic volumes. Sometimes Google will change the link for this tool so if you have difficulty getting this link to work, just do a Google search for "Google Keyword Tool." This tool is free and does a great job of recommending potential search terms.

Step 3) Download all of the keywords into an Excel spreadsheet by clicking on the download button.

Step 4) In your new Excel file, do a data sort of keywords with the highest traffic. To sort the data, you'll have to go to the data tab at the top and click sort. If you're having difficulties, do a Google search for sorting data in Excel. Ensure that you sort first by keywords with the highest monthly traffic volumes.

Once you've done all of this, select five to ten keywords toward the top of the list that you think are most relevant to your website.

Now that you have your initial search terms, we will want to determine how much competition there will be for these keywords. The Google Keyword Tool will provide its own competition estimate when you download the file. However, you should be aware that this estimate refers to the level of competition on the paid search side and isn't a true reflection of how competitive a search term will be when attempting to optimize your website for organic rankings.

Google gives priority to sites that are seen as authoritative, have been around a long time, and are consistently creating and publishing useful information for their users. Therefore, if you do a search on your target keywords and see a bunch of sites appear that adhere closely to that description—such as Wikipedia or the *New York Times*—it's going to be very difficult to make progress with even the best strategies in place.

When determining search term competition, there are plenty of great SEO tools out on the market. One that I tend to use quite a bit and highly recommend is Moz (**www.moz.com**) While this tool does cost some money, Moz offers a free thirty-day trial. This Seattle-based software company has acquired a particularly strong reputation in the SEO space and they have a very active community that's always happy to answer SEO-related questions. This software will help you identify opportunities, while the community will put you in touch with experienced professionals who can answer questions and provide insights into SEO. If you do decide to use Moz on an ongoing basis, you'll only need the minimum level of service, currently $100/month. Though, as mentioned, the company does offer a free one-month trial if you want to explore their tool set before making any type of commitment. Also important to note, you do not have to be a paying member of Moz to benefit from the information available on their blog. So feel free to check out their blog at any point if you have specific questions about SEO or simply want to check out what's new in the industry.

Before going any further, it's important to understand that there are some great SEO tools out there to help you reach your online goals. While Moz is one of the more prominent resources featured throughout this book, my goal is to showcase the value that tools like this can bring to the table when working on your search engine presence. Later in this book, there will be other tools mentioned that provide similar features to Moz. I want to give you some insights into what these tools can do for you and then give you the ability to go out and find the tools that will work best for your purposes.

With regard to these SEO tools, the strategies outlined in this book could absolutely be done for free, without having to spend any money on software or tools. If you would like to research keyword competitiveness with a tool that offers a free version, you can utilize WebSEO Analytics here: **http://www.webseoanalytics.com/free/seo-tools/keyword-difficulty.php.**

The software tools that I highlight throughout this book are designed to help with these SEO activities while speeding things up. However, you should never spend money on anything related to search engine optimization unless you can afford it and feel you will receive a future payback from your investment. With this in mind, let's continue with our SEO keyword research.

Once you have an idea about which search terms you want to target based on relevancy and potential traffic, go to the Keyword Analysis tool in Moz or the free tool at WebSEO Analytics.

Once at the Keyword Analysis tool, you're going to input the search terms to get an idea of how competitive they are on the major search engines so that you will get some idea around competition levels such as this:

Not All Search Terms Are Created Equal

Keywords	Keyword Difficulty Score	Local Search Volume	Global Monthly Search Volume
seattle advertising agencies	46	1,600	1,600
marketing firms seattle	47	720	880
marketing firms in seattle	51	720	880
seo seattle search engine optimization	50	880	1,000
seattle marketing company	49	880	1,000

The difficulty score takes into account the authority and page rank of sites that are currently enjoying strong rankings for our targeted search terms, along with how many websites are going after the same keywords and a few other additional factors. In my opinion, any search term that has a difficulty score in the low to medium range should be okay to go after initially. With Moz, this would be any term with a competition score under 50. However, the lower a search term's score, the better, as it will be easier to get increased rankings. In the event that some of your targeted search terms are too competitive, it would be advisable to start with some of the other search terms from your initial list. After all, the goal is to increase your search traffic as quickly as possible, and choosing the right search terms to target is a key factor in this goal.

Once you've found the right combination of search terms based on traffic potential and overall competition, these will be the keywords we'll target initially with our search engine optimization efforts. This list will be constantly changing as we obtain rankings, but this is where we'll start. Once you obtain strong rankings on your first set of keywords, repeat the process and go after more search terms!

To go a step further, another useful tool for identifying potential search terms is SpyFu. This company can provide invaluable competitive insight. There are both free and paid versions; the free version will be more than ample for your needs when it comes to keyword evaluation.

First, navigate to spyfu.com and input a term you're considering. For example, if I wanted to research the term "buy a car" on SpyFu, I would receive the following information in the organic search ranking analysis:

Rank (Change)	URL	Domain	Domain Strength	Est. Clicks/ Month
1 (--)	http://www.autotrader.com	autotrader.com	70	961
2 (1 ↑)	http://www.carmax.com	carmax.com	58	490
3 (-1 ↓)	http://www.cars.com/ for-sale/	cars.com	71	331
4 (6 ↑)	http://autos.yahoo.com/ newcars/buy.html	yahoo.com	89	250
5 (--)	http://auto.howstuffworks. com	howstuffworks. com	78	202
6 (-2 ↓)	http://money.cnn.com/ magazines.html	cnn.com	83	169
7 (2 ↑)	http://www.edmunds.com/ car-buying.html	edmunds.com	75	145
8 (--)	http://www.fool.com/car. htm	fool.com	73	128
9 (3 ↑)	http://www.consumer.ftc. gov	ftc.gov	70	114
10 (-3 ↓)	http://chicagotribune.com/ classified/	chicagotribune. com	80	103

As you can see from this search, I would be able to identify the top websites currently ranking for the search term in question, the ranking increase or decrease that each of these sites has recently experienced, the strength of domain for each of these websites, and the estimated clicks/month that each website is driving from the search term in question. This is powerful information that can also be used to identify the search terms that make the most sense to target.

Our main focus with this type of research is to find the right organic search terms. By organic search terms, I mean search terms that naturally rank on the search engines as opposed to search terms that have been bought. When you do a search on Google, you'll typically see sponsored searches at the top and right-hand side of the screen that have actually been purchased. Our focus is on the rest of the search results that can be had for free!

Here's an illustration to demonstrate the difference:

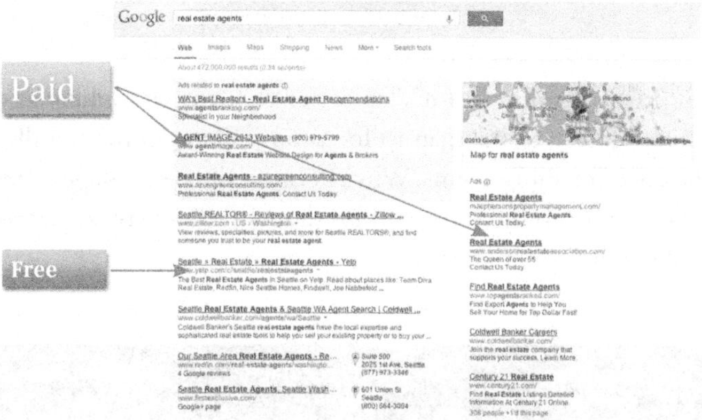

Throughout my career in marketing, one thing I've always found interesting is the fact that 80 percent of time, money, and resources spent on increasing search engine visibility is focused on paid search. However, 80 percent of all search engine traffic actually comes from the organic searches, which can be obtained for free!

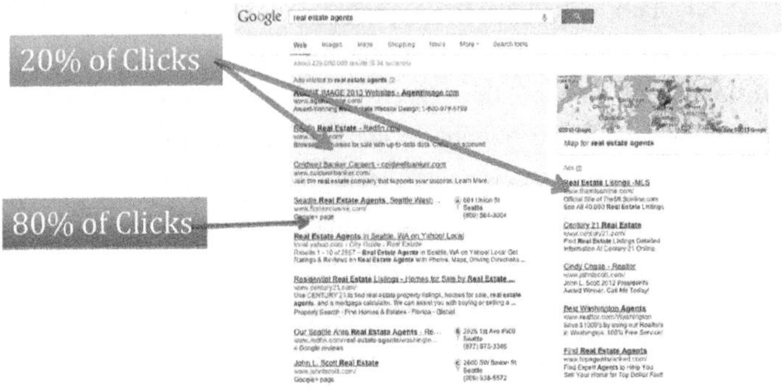

Keep in mind that it's far better to focus on ranking at the top for fewer terms than to focus on ranking in the middle of the pack for more terms. Why? Because the percentage of traffic that goes to the top positions dramatically increases as your ranking improves.

Resulting Position	Average Percentage of Clicks	Difference in Clicks
#1	42.1%	N/A
#2	11.9%	3.5X Less
#3	8.5%	4.9X Less
#4	6.1%	6.9X Less
#5	4.9%	8.5X Less
#6	4.1%	10.4X Less
#7	3.4%	12.3X Less
#8	3.0%	14.0X Less
#9	2.8%	14.8X Less
#10	3.0%	14.1X Less
#11-20	10.1%	N/A
#21-1,000	1.2%	N/A

Data Courtesy of Moz

Identifying the right search terms to target is the most important thing you can do to help ensure your success on the search engines. If you don't have the right search terms to target, it is highly unlikely that you end up getting much value from the rest of your efforts. It will be more difficult to make progress in the rankings, and even if you do make progress, there may not be much search traffic for you to benefit from. Focusing on the right keywords is the motor that will drive this car forward.

With this in mind, it would only be fitting for me to include some other highly regarded keyword tools in order to provide some additional options available for keyword research:

- Market Samurai ($97/one time and offers free trial)
  http://www.marketsamurai.com

  Market Samurai generates keywords and traffic statistics based on Google search query data and provides a range of additional analytics and tools. Some of the more popular tools include the Rank Tracker, which allows you to track all of your keywords, the Keyword Research Tool, which helps you find relevant keywords and conduct an in-depth analysis, and the SEO Competition Tool, which allows you to analyze the top ten sites ranking on your target keywords.

- Word Tracker ($69/month and offers free trial)
  http://www.wordtracker.com

  Word Tracker generates keywords and traffic statistics based on searches performed across all the main search engines, including Google and Bing. It uses a database of over 330 million search terms, which it updates weekly.

- Keyword Discovery ($69.95/month and offers free trial) **http://keyworddiscovery.com**

  Keyword Discovery generates keywords and traffic statistics from over two hundred search engines worldwide and claims to have the largest keyword database, containing nearly thirty-eight billion searches. Keyword Discovery imports the search engines' search logs into its database or collects samples from its user panel and other sources. Data is collected daily, but due to the size of the index, the database is updated monthly.

Finding the right set of keywords to target with your search engine optimization efforts is the first and most important step in getting to that very important spot at the top of Google. So make sure to get it right and you will be well on your way to achieving success online.

➢ SEO Challenge #1: Keyword Development

Use the Google KeywordTool to find ten keywords that have at least one thousand monthly searches and are relevant to your target audience. How many monthly searches does your top keyword receive?

➢ Tools And Tricks

Keyword Research

- **Google Keyword Tool (https://adwords.google.com)**

Go to the free Google Keyword Tool and find search terms that are receiving high volumes of interest every single month. This is an incredible resource for keyword research.

- **Market Samurai (http://www.marketsamurai.com)**

Generate keywords and traffic statistics based on Google search query data. The Keyword Research Tool can help you find relevant keywords and conduct an in-depth analysis.

- **Word Tracker (http://www.wordtracker.com)**

Generate keywords and traffic statistics based on searches performed across all of the main search engines, including Google and Bing, by using this database of over three hundred million search terms.

- **Keyword Discovery (http://keyworddiscovery.com)**

Generate keywords and traffic statistics from over two hundred search engines worldwide with software that claims to have the largest keyword database, containing nearly thirty-eight billion searches.

- **Competitive Research Moz (www.moz.com)**

Use the keyword analysis tool to figure out how competitive the specific search terms may be. Don't spend your time optimizing for search terms that are too difficult to effectively acquire rankings.

- **WebSEO Analytics (http://www.webseoanalytics.com)**

Use the keyword difficulty tool to speed up the keyword research process by screening the Keyword List and excluding the terms that will be difficult to achieve top page positioning. It will help you select the terms for which you have a good chance to rank.

- **SpyFu (www.spyfu.com)**

Research keywords and find the search terms that are driving the most traffic to competitor websites on a monthly basis.

Chapter 3

Website Success in Excess

After you've selected your target search terms, you will need to make your site more search-engine-friendly. There are a few key areas you'll want to focus on when creating or tweaking your website.

- **Avoid using Flash for your site**
  Google's robots are not very sophisticated; they primarily pick up on content and links but not much else. Building your site in Flash will significantly reduce the content you're able to include and could hurt your ability to rank on the search engines. Therefore, it is recommended that your site be built without relying on Flash.

- **Include a sitemap on your website**
  A sitemap will typically help your site to be better organized for both your audience and the search engine robots. Having a sitemap will therefore assist the search engine robots to quickly crawl your site.

- **Include internal linking throughout your site**
  Internal linking can be a contributing factor to increased rankings. Therefore, it's important to include links within your site to other areas of the site wherever possible.

- **Use the target search terms on your site**
  If there's a search term you want to rank for, you must incorporate it into the text on your website at least a few times. I would recommend that you use your target keywords within the first twenty-five words and the last twenty-five words on your page. I would also recommend that you bold your target keyword at least once. Often times, when your site is crawled by Google, their robots will scan it and put more emphasis on the beginning and the end of the page.

  Incorporating your target search terms into the page multiple times is commonly referred to as keyword density and can help your efforts as long as it is used with moderation. However, it is very important that you ensure the page provides a good user experience. If not, the visitors you start to attract will leave your site immediately and all of this work won't do you much good. Always keep in mind user experience when optimizing your site.

- **Use the most important search terms in your page title (Google recommends using less than *65 characters*)**
  Search engines rely heavily upon page titles to determine relevancy. You should always include your top keywords in the page title.

- **Use image alt tags on your images**
  Search engine spiders are fairly unsophisticated and aren't able to identify images. These tags will help the search engines understand what the images represent on your website.

- **Incorporate important search terms in header tags**
  Businesses often overlook header tags as a place to highlight important keywords. Placing search terms within header tags increases rankings and relevancy.
  Here's an example of areas on your website that these HTML tags would impact:

Optimize Header Tag - Employing targeted keywords in the H1 tag has shown to correlate with higher rankings. It's also considered a best practice for accessibility and to describe a page's content.

Keyword Usage in Document - Text content is very important for modern SEO. In order to optimize your chances of ranking higher for the targeted keyword(s), I highly recommend using multiple targeted keyword(s) on your site.

Add Image AltTags - Keyword usage in the alt attribute of an image employed on a page is surprisingly positively correlated with good rankings. It also helps considerably with image searches.

Other areas that you will want to focus on in order to make your website SEO-friendly include:

- **Leverage the meta description (Google recommends using less than *156 characters*)**

This is a place to briefly list what your site is about, what products you offer, what areas you service, and other vital information. It will impact your website's description on the search engines, so it's important to get it right. It's the first impression you leave with a prospective customer.

- **Avoid using meta keywords**

Many website owners still rely on meta keywords in their attempts to make their websites search-engine-friendly. Search engines largely ignore the meta keywords tag in their ranking algorithms. While it technically won't harm your rankings, it can give competitors insight into what search terms you are targeting in your SEO efforts. Why would you ever want to help the competition?

Courtesy of the folks at Moz, here is an example of what a perfectly optimized website page will look like for the keyword "chocolate donuts":

Recommended Page Title: Chocolate Donuts | Mary's Bakery

Recommended Meta Description: Mary's Bakery's chocolate donuts are possibly the most delicious, perfectly formed, flawlessly chocolate donuts ever made.

Recommended Page URL: **http://marysbakery.com/chocolate-donuts**

The "Perfectly" Optimized Page

(for the example keyword phrase "chocolate donuts")

Page Title: Chocolate Donuts | Mary's Bakery

Meta Description: Mary's Bakery's chocolate donuts are possibly the most delicious, perfectly formed, flawlessly chocolately donuts ever made.

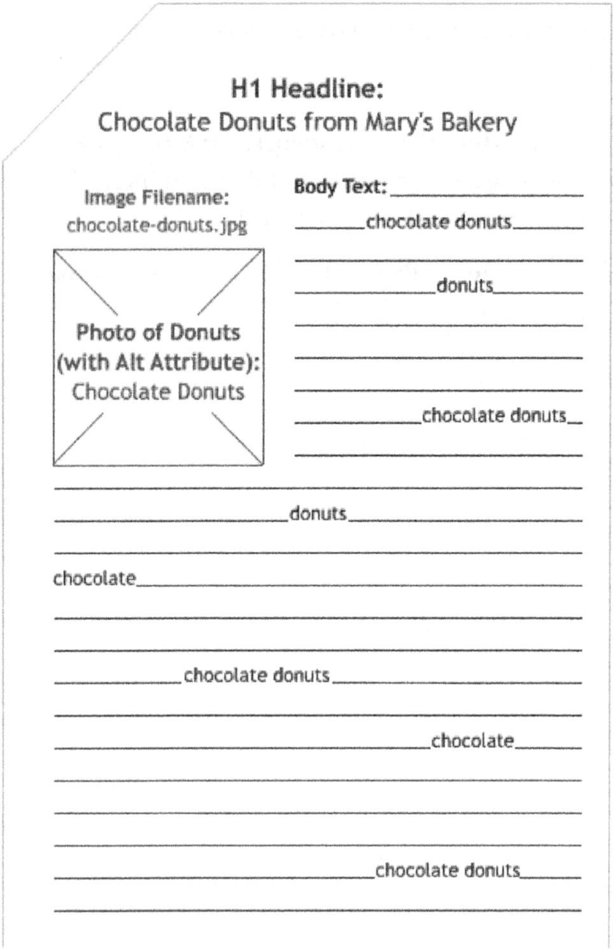

Fill out the header, title, and meta tags properly and include keywords in the content and image descriptions and your site will be ready to be found by the search engines.

When it comes to website development, there is an organization that sets the standards for how websites are supposed to be structured. If you want to take your website to the next level, you can consult with the World Wide Web Consortium, or W3C **(http://www.w3.org)** as it is commonly referred to, in order to ensure that you are meeting all the proper guidelines.

I also recommend that you implement Google Webmaster Tools, which provides visibility into how your website is viewed by the search engines. Here's why it's important to incorporate Google Webmaster Tools:

1. Google will list all the pages on your site that it has indexed so that you can ensure your website is being recognized by Google.

2. Google employs a bot whose job it is to crawl your site and index you according to what it finds. If your site doesn't link everything clearly (thus the recommendation for a sitemap), Google might miss a couple of your pages and that would not be a good thing. By incorporating Google Webmaster Tools, you'll have the ability to tell Google where all of your individual pages can be found.

3. In the event that you have some pages you don't want Google to find, you will have the ability to tell them not to index you. With Google Webmaster Tools, you can be sure that web pages that may be somewhat

embarrassing or not ready for prime time aren't suddenly finding themselves in the searches.

4. While there are some other tools I recommend in this book to track your incoming links, Google Webmaster Tools will allow you to see how many links are being directed to your site that Google is able to identify. After all, it can't hurt to check this information directly from the source that matters most given how important these links are to your overall potential to rank in the search engines.

5. You can use Webmaster Tools to get Google to index your images. If your site has great images incorporated throughout, then you can use them to enhance your search engine visibility. Just set up the enhanced image search in Webmaster Tools and make sure you've included the image alt tags with relevant descriptions and keywords.

6. Another important feature of Webmaster Tools is a content analysis tool. It will highlight any issues that may make it difficult for Google to crawl and index your site. This can provide a very powerful to-do list when it comes to improving your onsite optimizations.

There are other reasons to incorporate Google Webmaster Tools, but these are some of the more important ones, and I think you get the point.

Now that we know why it's a good idea to set up Google Webmaster Tools, let's move on to how one would actually go about setting up Google Webmaster Tools.

Here is a step-by-step breakdown:

Step 1 – If you don't already have a Google account, such as Gmail, you will need to create one here: https://accounts.google.com/NewAccount. If you do already have a Gmail account, skip this step.

Step 2 – Go to **https://www.google.com/webmasters/tools** and register for a Google Webmaster Tools account. Then sign in so that you can set it up.

Step 3 — Once signed in, you can add your website address and click the Add Site button.

Step 4 – After this, you will be asked to verify your site. Since you can only set up websites on Google Webmaster Tools that you personally own, you will be required to prove that you own the site before you can be fully up and running. The most common form of verification is to download an HTML file that Google provides to you and then upload the file onto your server. Once you confirm that the file has been uploaded by clicking on the verify button, you are good to go.

Now that you're set up on Google Webmaster Tools, you'll be able to see all kinds of information about your site to ensure that Google is finding you in the way that you intend.

To check on the overall effectiveness of your website for SEO purposes, Moz has a useful tool as well.

When you log into Moz, you can go to the **On-Page Grader** tool to check on the overall SEO effectiveness of your current website.

Enter your target search term along with your domain name. Once you submit this information, you'll be given a grade for how successfully your website is optimized, along with areas of opportunity to better optimize your site.

You'll be presented with a detailed page analysis and recommended fixes for any issues that may exist. Some of the areas that this tool will evaluate on your website include critical factors such as:

- Accessibility to search engines
- Keyword usage in document
- Keyword usage in the page title

Other less critical factors that this tool will also analyze include:

- Keyword usage in image alt attribute tags
- Whether there are sufficient quantities of keywords in your content
- Proper keyword usage in the URL
- Keyword usage in your H1 Tag
- Keyword usage in meta description
- Appropriate URL lengths

If you're not quite sure what some of this means, every recommendation comes with a full explanation on what the recommendation means for your website.

If you're looking for a free tool that can help you to evaluate your website, you can check out WebSEO Analytics here: **http://www.webseoanalytics.com/free/seo-tools/web-seo-analysis.php.**

Use the resources at your disposal to make sure proper tags and keywords are being utilized and you will ensure that your site is in a strong position to be found on the search engines for the search terms you are targeting.

Now that you have a good idea of how you can impact your ability to get the search engines to discover your website, it will be very important to ensure that you set up your website in a way that encourages a strong call to action. By call to action, I am referring to the action you are attempting to get the visitor to take when they come to your website.

The reality is that your website will most likely exist for a specific purpose. While there are many types of websites out there with various intentions, every website should strive to invoke some type of action from the visitor. If you're promoting a cause, you can collect e-mail addresses on your website to keep people updated on the progress you're making. If you're promoting a service business, you can prominently display your phone number and e-mail address with the intention of getting individuals to contact you to schedule an appointment. And if you're selling a product on your site, you will want to make it as easy as possible to buy from you because the easier it is for your customers to buy, the more likely it is that they *will* buy.

Take a look at this website (**www.medicalmarketing-help.org**) which was set up to promote a marketing class:

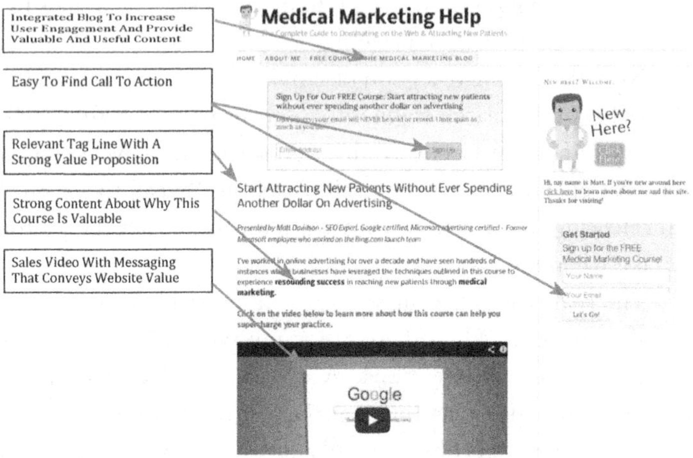

It's important to note that this website was set up with the intention of getting visitors to provide their e-mail addresses to receive marketing lessons delivered to their in-box every few days. With this purpose in mind, the website was designed to show in a compelling way how these lessons can help users reach their own goals, and to make it easy for visitors to discern what action the website is attempting to get them to take (i.e., providing their e-mail addresses). By offering a strong case for why visitors would want to provide their e-mail address and making it extremely easy for them to do so, this website has achieved a very strong conversion rate.

While there are many things that can impact a website's overall ability to turn a visitor into a customer, the main take-away here is that you will want to ensure that you are building a clean website that is easy to navigate and makes the following details very clear:

- What action you're trying to get the visitor to take

- What makes you the best option to help the visitor
- What about your business differentiates your site
- What specific services/products you are offering

When it comes to your website, there are two main things on which to focus your efforts. The first is to get your website found by the major search engines so that you can bring in as many visitors as possible who are interested in what you have to offer. The second is to ensure that your website is in a strong position to take meaningful advantage of this incoming traffic to help you accomplish the overall goals you have set for your website. By combining your focus in these two areas, you will ensure that you are in a great position to experience success online.

➢ **SEO Challenge #2: Onsite Optimization**

Install Google Webmaster Tools on your website. Then using the content analysis tool, check your site for any errors. Were there more or less errors than you had expected?

➢ **Tools And Tricks**

Website Optimization Analysis

- **Moz (www.moz.com)**

Receive graded on-page keyword targeting. Find out how well your pages are optimized for target keywords, and improve your site for the best performance possible with Moz's On-Page Optimization Report.

- **WebSEO Analytics (http://www.web-seoanalytics.com)**

This tool produces a full SEO report for a particular page or website, analyzes the most important SEO factors that are used by the major search engines and offers detailed diagnostics with all the errors and warnings that were found during the analysis.

- **Google Webmaster Tools (https://www.google.com/websmasters/tools)**

Receive detailed reports and information about your visibility on Google and how well your website is doing when it comes to getting crawled and indexed by the Google search engine.

Website Accessibility Reporting

- **World Wide Web Consortium (www.w3.org)**

Learn about common protocols and standards that can impact the ability to get your website noticed by the search engines.

Chapter 4

Linking Up: Safety in Numbers

Now that you've set up your site so the search engines know what you're about, it's time to let them know that you exist. How do you do this? Through links! Search engines highly value the quality and quantity of external websites linking to your website. Why is that, you ask? Because when a website links back to you, it's an indication that your site matters. A link is a sign that another website gives you its nod of approval.

When two graduate students originally founded Google, the idea for the search engine came from the fact that research papers were typically deemed more important when they were referenced by other external papers, researchers, etc. Essentially, the more references and mentions a research paper received, the higher the level of importance and value was typically placed on said research paper. If you think about it, links serve as these citations that once influenced the creation of Google.

But not all links are created equal. If CNN.com links to your site as a valuable resource for their audience, Google sees this as a high-quality recommendation. If Smalltimeautoshack.com links back to you, Google won't give it as much attention. And in the Internet world, attention is a good thing.

Courtesy of Moz, here's a graphic to demonstrate the importance of link building:

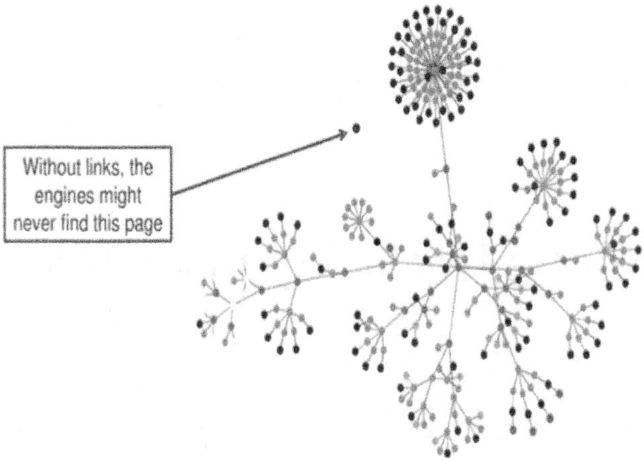

They call it the World Wide Web for a reason. There really is a web of sites continually pointing to each other to create groupings of relevant information. We live in an interconnected world. It has never been more important to get connected on the web with links flowing to your website.

Create your own "link destiny," so to speak, and put yourself light years ahead of the competition. Throughout the following chapters, I'll cover exactly how to go about becoming the link-acquiring machine that will help you get the online results you're after.

Chapter 5

Localize It: Location, Location, Location

Do you have a website or business that's focused on working with people in your neighborhood? Maybe you're a local dentist, handyman, or landscaper or you run a local restaurant or auto repair shop. You get the idea. Google has a completely different search result for these types of location-specific searches.

Try a Google search for the "best restaurants in Seattle" and you're likely to get results that look different than standard searches. They will typically have a Zagat score, Google Reviews and will include an address and phone number as well as incorporating a Google map listing.

If you're a local business or website, getting found on the local search engine rankings, which often include Google Maps pinpointing your location, will be critical in attracting customers in and around your community.

Map citations on the Internet assist search engines by helping them know more about your business or entity, such as your location, services, and hours of operation. These map citations can even include images.

So what is a citation exactly? A citation is where your business name and address are mentioned, or cited, on another website. Google crawls content across the web and anywhere they find a citation of your business, they give you credit toward their search engine rankings.

And how do you show up on these map searches? It all starts with creating a strong local profile. If you register your business on all of these sites, you will be well ahead of the game—and the competition.

Page Rank	Site	Website URL
9	Google Places	www.google.com/local/add/businessCenter
9	Bing Local	www.bing.com/local/
8	Yahoo! Local	www.listings.local.yahoo.com/
8	Merchant Circle	www.merchantcircle.com/signup/
8	Facebook Places	www.facebook.com/pages/create.php
8	Linked In	www.linkedin.com/company/add/show
7	Yelp	www.yelp.com/writeareview/newbiz
7	Seek It Local	www.seekitlocal.com/getlisted.aspx

Page Rank	Site	Website URL
7	Local.com	www.advertise.local.com/
6	Yellow Pages.com	www.adsolutions.att.com/ advertising/
6	Manta	www.manta.com/claim
6	White Pages	www.whitepages.com/listing
6	Super Pages	www.supermedia.com/ business-listings
6	InfoUSA	www.leads.infousa.com/ Landing/UpdateListing.aspx
6	Angie's List	www.business.angieslist.com/ Registration
6	Yellow Book	www.yellowbook360.com/ advertise/
6	City Search	www.citysearch.com/members/ login
6	Map Quest	www.listings.mapquest.com/ apps/listing
6	Four Square	www.foursquare.com/business/ merchants/claiming
6	City Squares	www.my.citysquares.com/search
6	Hot Frog	www.hotfrog.com/ AddYourBusiness.aspx
6	Biznik	www.biznik.com/members/ new

Page Rank	Site	Website URL
6	Kudzu	www.register.kudzu.com/packageSelect.do
5	Dex One	www.dexknows.com/info/build.asp
5	Match Point	www.providers.matchpoint.com/register.htm
5	Magic Yellow	www.magicyellow.com/add-your-business.cfm
5	Yellow Bot	www.yellowbot.com/signin
5	Think Local	www.thinklocal.com/Business-Signup.aspx
5	Biz Journal	www.businessdirectory.bizjournals.com/advertise
5	Local Eze	www.webapp.localeze.com/directory/search.aspx
4	Yellowee	www.yellowee.com/business/add
4	Mojo Pages	www.mojopages.com/biz/signup
4	Small Business Listings	www.smallbusinesslistings.com/signup.php
4	Zidster	www.zidster.com/forbiz.asp
3	City Slick	www.cityslick.net/reg.php
3	Tele Atlas	www.mapinsight.teleatlas.com/mapfeedback/index.php
3	Discover Our Town	www.discoverourtown.com/add/

Page Rank	Site	Website URL
3	US City	www.uscity.net/listmysite.html
3	Yellow Assistance	www.yellowassistance.com/frm-BusinessUpdate.aspx
3	Zipper Pages	www.zipperpages.com/adver-tise.html
2	Yippie	www.submit.yippie.biz/
2	Just Click Local	www.justclicklocal.com/user/join
2	Twibs	www.twibs.com/registration.php
2	Zip Web	www.zipweb.com/apply_login.php
2	Brown Book	www.brownbook.net/business/add/
2	Shop City	www.shopcity.com/add
1	Metro Bot	www.2.metrobot.com/
1	Best Deal On	www.bestdealon.com/addbusi-nesstodirectory.html
1	Infignos	www.infignos.com/addlisting/speedlist.cfm
1	Toll Free Directory	www.inter800.com/freelist.htm
1	Biz Highway	www.bizhwy.com/addlisting.php

On a side note, Google gives websites a PageRank between one and ten. The higher the PageRank, the more credibility a site will have when factored into Google's rankings. You can use this information when determining what sites you want to work with to obtain links to your site.

When filling out these profiles, you'll be asked to provide:

- Contact person
- Address
- E-mail
- Phone number
- Services
- Category of business
- Pictures of business
- Description of business

You can also include any other important details about your business. Some of these sites will offer a free or paid option of inclusion. You'll be fine if you only choose the free option as you build out these profiles.

Think you'll go crazy submitting your site to local directories over and over again? To avoid writer's cramp, there are companies out there that can help, such as **https://www.ubl.org**. Provide your information and, for a nominal fee, they'll post your site across dozens of local directories on your behalf.

I recommend checking on the directories to which they submit in order to ensure that all of the sites listed above are included. For the sites that are missing, you'll want to submit those manually if you choose to use UBL.

Also, be aware that most of these local directories have some type of verification process, such as calling your phone or sending you a postcard with a PIN code enclosed. The reason these sites implement a verification process is to prove that you actually exist at the location you have specified so that this information is as accurate as possible. Make sure you are receiving these verifications and responding to them so you can be assured that you are getting placement on these sites.

Now that you have your local profiles set up, what other factors will help your status as a local superstar?

Put simply, customer reviews, customer reviews, and more customer reviews. Reviews have become an increasingly important aspect of local searches for two reasons. First, reviews can actually have a positive impact on search rankings. Secondly, reviews will tremendously increase the percentage of searchers that click over to your website when they find you on Google. People love and trust reviews.

When you do a localized search on Google, you will notice a common trend. Those high-ranking websites all have a large number of Google reviews. So how do you get reviews? You ask for them.

It's imperative you make a serious effort to follow up with anyone who's used your services or products. I also recommend offering your customers an incentive to fill out the reviews. An incentive could be anything from a discount the next time they do business with you to a Starbucks gift card. After all, they're spending their own time to write a review for you. Every time I've made the effort to collect these reviews, it has paid off. I'll repeat—*every time.*

I recommend focusing primarily on collecting Google Places reviews since Google has a tremendous amount of users and gives preference to its own reviews. However, Google recently purchased Zagat and is including those reviews in their searches for relevant categories as well. Yelp is another service that can be a robust referral source for business if you have a strong profile set up with lots of reviews. While Yelp won't play a big part in your search engine rankings, it will make sense to focus on it once you've fully established yourself on Google as the local superstar that you are. Yelp can serve as a tremendous referral source on top of the traffic you're receiving from Google.

Here's a sample e-mail I've sent that seems to work well:

REVIEW US ON GOOGLE PLACES

At [name of business here], we are always excited to be at your service.

One of the top compliments we can receive is a testimonial from you! Google Places is where most people search for local services online, and we'd love it if you can go there and write a little something about us. It's a very simple process and will help us tremendously in getting the word out!

We really appreciate your support and thank you for being a part of our family!

CLICK HERE
to post your review

If you're not currently collecting your customers' e-mail addresses as part of your business process, you should be. If you're looking for a reliable company to help with the sending of these e-mail requests, I recommend Mail Chimp (**www.mailchimp.com**) since it offers inexpensive services and a ridiculous amount of useful information about the e-mails you send through them. Currently, they offer a free service for your first two thousand subscribers, so there is really nothing to lose by trying them out. Mail Chimp can tell you how many e-mails were sent, which e-mails were read, how many users clicked on your Google Places page, and more.

Once you get your local profiles filled out and your review request process in place, you'll be in a great position to start driving some serious local search engine traffic.

- **SEO Challenge #3: Getting Local with Google Places**
  Sign up for a Google Places page and optimize for the location of your business and the services you offer. If you already have a Places page, optimize it for the keywords you selected in Challenge #1. How long did it take for Google to verify your listing?

- **Tools And Tricks**

  Local Directory Submissions

  - **Universal Business Listing (www.ubl.org)**
  Provides a fast means for businesses of all sizes to get listed on all of the major search engines, online yellow pages, social networks, and mapping sites.

  E-mail Outreach
  - **Mail Chimp (www.mailchimp.com)**
  Mail Chimp offers a fantastic e-mail marketing solution to manage contacts, send e-mails and track results. Better yet, the first two thousand contacts are free. If you're looking to do any e-mail outreach with your customers, this tool is highly recommended.

Chapter 6

The Unique Content Universe

Search engines highly value unique content, such as a newly written article or blog entry related to your business and posted to the World Wide Web. The engines want their searchers to find material relevant for their searches, and they will often prioritize websites that continue to put out a steady flow of unique content. In fact, creating and distributing well-written and valuable content is such a critical component of search engine optimization that it should serve as the backbone for your entire strategy.

In terms of generating new content, you have two options. Option one is to write the content yourself. After all, you know your business better than anyone else. Option two is to pay a contractor or company to write the content on your behalf. More on this later in the chapter.

There are multiple options when it comes to distributing the content you create. You can post it on a blog that you control. You can post it to an outside blog as a guest blogger. You have the option to post the article to an article directory. Or you can submit the article to a website owner you come across who is looking for the type of content you are writing. Just make sure the owner is willing to provide you with a link in exchange for your contribution. The goal is to create links back to your site, driving increased rankings and new traffic.

Another option when it comes to content is to submit your material as a press release. This can help create brand awareness and generate an increase in incoming links. One thing to keep in mind when writing a press release is that you want to keep the content newsworthy. This means writing about a new product launch or new service. Keep the press release limited to something of significance to create as much buzz as possible. Obviously, this is easier for some types of businesses than others, but I'm sure if you get creative, you'll find something you can use to craft a stellar press release.

When it comes to distributing the press release, there are plenty of options for getting the word out. One of the biggest PR distribution sites is called PRWeb (**www.prweb.com**). However, it can get a bit expensive if you're just starting out and not quite sure if PR distribution is worthy of your time just yet. With this in mind, there is another great service that can help you distribute your press releases for free, PRLog (**www.prlog.org**). Feel free to check out both of these services to determine which one makes the most sense for your website.

When contributing your newly created content, it's critical that you include links back to your site within the articles. Each distribution site is different, so pay attention to instructions when doing this.

While press releases provide a great resource for building awareness and generating incoming links, you will have to be careful to not send out press releases so frequently that they lose their value. With this in mind, you will want to focus the majority of your content creation on article writing.

Here is an extensive list of article submission sites you can use with the intention of submitting the unique content you've written:

Page Rank	Site	Website URL
8	Hub Pages	www.hubpages.com/signin/
8	Squidoo	www.squidoo.com/member/login
8	Ezine Articles	www.ezinearticles.com/submit/?
8	Technorati	www.technorati.com/account/login/
7	Suite 101	www.suite101.com/signin
7	The Free Library	www.secure.farlex.com/Login.aspx
7	Article Pros	www.articlepros.com/login
6	Gather	www.gather.com/login.action
6	Bright Hub	www.secure.brighthub.com/tools/login
6	Self Growth	www.selfgrowth.com/user
6	Sooper Articles	www.sooperarticles.com/author-login.html

Page Rank	Site	Website URL
6	Article Base	www.articlesbase.com/login
5	Buzzle	www.buzzle.com/admin/login.asp
5	Idea Marketers	www.ideamarketers.com/login.cfm
5	Triond	www.triond.com/login
5	Article Trader	www.articletrader.com/login/
5	Isnare	www.isnare.com/login.php
5	Article City	www.articlecity.com/free_article_submission.php
5	Article Blast	www.articleblast.com/option,com_comprofiler/
5	Article Dashboard	www.articledashboard.com/login.php
5	Write Stuff	www.WryteStuff.com/LoginV2.asp
5	Article Alley	www.login.articlealley.com/
4	Info Barrel	www.infobarrel.com/signup.php
4	Pub Articles	www.pubarticles.com/members/login.php
4	Article Rich	www.articlerich.com/login2submitart.php
4	Article Cube	www.articlecube.com/login

Page Rank	Site	Website URL
4	Article Factory	www.articlesfactory.com/submit.html
4	Article Compilation	www.articlecompilation.com/login.php
4	Snipsly	www.snipsly.com/write-an-article/
4	Article Click	www.articleclick.com/sign-up
4	1-888 Articles	www.1888articles.com/login.html
4	Article Monkey	www.articlemonkeys.com/login.php
4	Artipot	www.artipot.com/info/submit-articles.htm
4	Article Snatch	www.articlesnatch.com/login2submitart.php
4	E Article	www.e-articles.info/e-submit-articles.htm
3	Go Articles	www.goarticles.com/members/
3	Ezine Mark	www.ezinemark.com/login/
3	Amazines	www.amazines.com/register.cfm
3	ABC Article Directory	www.abcarticledirectory.com/login2submitart.php
3	Street Articles	www.streetarticles.com/login
3	Article Biz	www.articlebiz.com/submit_article/

Page Rank	Site	Website URL
3	Ewagz	www.ewagz.com/submit-article/
3	Syn Articles	www.synarticles.com/account/act/login
3	Article Info	www.articleinfo.org/login-2submitart.php
3	Talkin Mince	www.talkinmince.com/login.php
3	Article Feeder	www.articlefeeder.com/submit_articles
3	Acme Articles	www.acmearticles.com/submit-articles/
3	Four PX Articles	www.fourpxarticles.com/?action=login
3	Tiny Article	www.tinyarticle.com/login.php
3	Article Bliss	www.articlebliss.com/signup.php
3	Directory Blog	www.directoryblog.org/submit_article.php
2	Article Cell	www.articlecell.com/login.php
2	Article Motron	www.articlemotron.com/login2submitart.php
2	Article Mania	www.article-mania.com/signup.php

Page Rank	Site	Website URL
2	Content Caboodle	www.contentcaboodle.com/submit/
2	Article Wagon	www.articlewagon.com/login2submitart.php
2	Freebie Article	www.freebie-articles.com/login.php
2	MX Get	www.articles.mxget.com/login.php
2	Niche Content Articles	www.niche-content-articles.com/login.php
2	Article Cabinet	www.articlecabi.net/submit/
2	Article Snare	www.articlesnare.com/submitarticle.htm
2	Submitted Article	www.submittedarticle.com/login.php
2	Article Trunk	www.articletrunk.com/login2submitart.php
1	Article County	www.articlecounty.com/index.php?page=login
1	Best Article Directory	www.bestarticledir.com/?ptype=submition
1	Article Cue	www.articlecue.com/login.php
1	Article Yard	www.articleyard.com/user/register

The major search engines, like Google, respect these sites and most will typically allow you to place links back to your site within your articles. Simply set up a profile and post. It's a fairly straightforward process and can have a huge impact on rankings.

If you'd like to see a sample article that I've created for one of my campaigns, you can check out this article:

http://ezinearticles.com/?Medical-Specialization-Is-Becoming-The-Way-Of-The-Future&id=7400191

As you can see from this article, there is a link embedded at the bottom of the article for a search term that I would like to target for increased search engine rankings. The anchor text is the visible, clickable text in a hyperlink. A hyperlink (or link) is a word, group of words, or image that you can click on to jump to another document. The words contained in the anchor text can determine the ranking that the page will receive by search engines because these types of links will help the search engine identify the target website as relevant for that term.

Here is the code that would be used to properly insert an anchor text link:

<a href="http://**www.medicalmarketinghelp.org**/">**Medical Marketing**</a>

By using this HTML code, the term "medical marketing" can be placed in a blog or article as a link text with the link pointing to the website URL: **http://www.medicalmarketinghelp.org.** This serves to inform the search engines that the article is about medical marketing while at the same time building a stronger link profile around a valuable search term.

You may be asking yourself, who has the time to write all these articles? Not to worry, as there are some solutions for that as well.

There are services available to assist with article writing. I'll warn you that they typically won't pen a journalistic masterpiece about your industry, so I highly recommend you spend some time writing content yourself if at all possible.

For about $30, you'll typically receive five articles that you can publish across article sites and on your blog.

When pressed for time, here are some services that can provide you with content for your SEO activities:

- 99centarticles.com
- articleninjas.com
- articlesontap.com
- ccarticles.com
- myarticleexpress.com

There's another service that can work well for this type of content writing called iWriter (**http://www.iwriter.com**). The good thing about iWriter is that you can order individual articles, set the price you wish to pay, and reject any articles that don't meet your standards. In that way, you can be assured that you are only paying for articles that you feel are up to your criteria. If you're short on time, it could definitely be worth giving this service a try since you have so much control over which articles to use in your SEO campaigns.

If these article-writing companies don't meet your approval, you can also look into hiring a part-time content writer. There are a couple of sites you can use to hire a content writer on a per-project or hourly basis. The two biggest sites with the most talent available are Elance (**www.elance.com**) and oDesk (**www.odesk.com**). On these sites, you can review vendors' past jobs and customer feedback and engage these potential content writers via e-mail or Skype before you actually hire them. Also, you'll have the ability to set up an account with Elance or oDesk so that the contractor doesn't get paid until the job is completed. The other nice thing about these networks is that they make it very easy to replace a contractor who isn't meeting expectations. These services have done a great job of limiting the risk and exposure involved with hiring an inexpensive contractor for content-writing purposes.

One caveat: it's very important that you don't publish these articles multiple times as the search engines will penalize you for duplication. They will know. One article should equal one submission.

With this in mind, I would like to quickly cover something that is a bit controversial in the SEO world. Quite a few SEO professionals engage in a process known as article spinning, which involves taking a well-written and informative article and replacing the main content with various synonyms. Thus, the article is essentially saying the same thing while changing enough words to make the search engines view the spun version of the article as though it were a unique article.

Now, this technique is technically considered "black hat," meaning that it is frowned upon by the major search engines. As someone writing a book on the proper way to market a website through SEO, I can't advocate that anyone go out and engage in article spinning. However, I feel as though I do have a responsibility to mention its existence given that it is so widely used by such a large number of SEO professionals.

Article spinning is a hot-button issue in the SEO community, and there are two sides of the argument. The first is that article spinning is a bad thing for the industry and its only purpose is to spam various websites with content that is passed off as unique but isn't. Opponents of article spinning argue that the practice does a disservice across the Internet because it floods websites with content that isn't strong enough to get picked up on its own and shared virally. These critics also argue that it goes against Google's guidelines, which can create problems down the line if Google ever detects that your website engages in article spinning.

The side that believes that article spinning is an acceptable practice will argue that Google's robots aren't sophisticated enough to determine great content from poor content and that it's the faulty system that created the need for article spinning in the first place. After all, if Ford takes the trouble to put together a great commercial, the company will buy airtime on every major network to air it. These individuals argue that article spinning has a similar effect, maximizing the reach of great content that was so painstakingly written by the website owner.

I believe both sides have a valid argument. My intent here is not to choose a side but to simply give you as much information as possible so you can make your own informed decision about how you would like to proceed with your content distribution efforts.

Google has made quite a few changes in the past year to their algorithm, changes that appear to be designed to address this issue. While these updates connote cute furry animals with names such as Panda and Penguin, make no mistake about their purpose. For those who haven't heard of Panda or Penguin before, these are a recent set of Google algorithm changes designed to discourage website owners from engaging in less than reputable activities to get their sites to the top of the Google search engine.

The Panda update is essentially a filter to stop sites with poor-quality content from working their way into Google's top search results. The Penguin update was created to better catch sites that spam the Google search results, especially those sites that are buying links or obtaining them through networks designed specifically to boost search engine rankings. I have not covered these Google shifts in much detail throughout this book since all of the strategies outlined in this book are in line with the website behavior that Google is encouraging. However, given this issue's impact on the SEO community, it makes sense to at least make you aware of it.

These algorithm changes are designed to encourage legitimate link building and incentivize website owners to create communities to share information, as opposed to spinning articles and sending them out to a bunch of different websites. While these shifts in Google's algorithms have thrown some SEO professionals for a loop, they don't appear to have completely eliminated article spinning. I am a firm believer that article spinning will cease to exist if/when Google legitimately makes changes that limit any positive impact these activities may currently enjoy. However, given the number of SEO professionals still using this technique, it's my belief that this hasn't fully happened yet.

While I don't specifically advocate the use of article spinning, it's important to at least acknowledge its existence and current role in SEO. I've been asked about article spinning by multiple clients and I want to ensure that you are armed with the right information in the event you come across article spinning in your own research. Although I'm not encouraging the use of article spinning, I wanted to make mention of it since it is widely known throughout the SEO community and is currently being used by some marketers in the industry.

In the event you choose to try your hand at article spinning, the best tool on the market for that is called The Best Spinner (**www.thebestspinner.com**). You set up your article in The Best Spinner, and it then creates different versions of it by replacing words throughout the article with synonyms. I will warn you that the tool isn't very sophisticated in determining the context of your words, so you will absolutely want to review the article prior to finalizing the spun versions. For example, if I were to write an article about search engine optimization, the tool would most likely recommend replacing the word engine with motor. Obviously, my article would not sound very professional or informative if it were written entirely about search motor optimization. Once an article is spun into different versions, marketers using this technique will then place the spun versions onto various article sites and pass them off as unique content.

Keep in mind that the goal with content creation is to get other sites to pick up your articles because the content is so interesting and valuable they want to share it with their audience. In turn, that audience will then share your content with other people and thereby drive natural links back to your website.

With the changes currently taking place at the major search engines, creating valuable content that makes you a thought leader in your space has become the most important thing you can do to influence your link-building efforts. So make sure you're putting out good content and the rest should ultimately take care of itself. In this way, the content you distribute will serve as a strong link-acquisition machine for your SEO efforts.

- **SEO Challenge #4: Article Submission**
  Sign up for an account with Ezine Articles. Next, write an article that is between 550–700 words about a keyword you chose in Challenge #1. Then include an anchor link in the author resource box that links back to your website. Finally, submit the article to Ezine under the appropriate category. How long did it take the Ezine editors to approve your article?

- **Tools And Tricks**

Press Release Submissions

- **PRWeb (www.prweb.com)**

A great option for press release distribution that can help you create buzz, increase online visibility, and drive website traffic.

- **PRLog (www.prlog.org)**

PRLog is another great press release distribution service that can help increase traffic and visibility. However, unlike PRWeb, this service is free to use, which makes it a cost-effective option for anyone looking to get the word out with a press release.

Content Writing Services

These services can provide quality article writing and web content for a very low price. If you're in need of content to help market your website and are short on time, these services can be a great option.

- **iWriter (www.iwriter.com)**
- **99 Cent Articles (www.99centarticles.com)**
- **Article Ninjas (www.articleninjas.com)**
- **Articles on Tap (www.articlesontap.com)**
- **CC Articles (www.ccarticles.com)**

Hiring A Content Writer

Businesses can use these websites to post jobs, search for freelance professionals, and solicit proposals. You can evaluate the contractors applying for the job by reviewing qualifications, work history, ratings, portfolios, and skill test scores.

- **Elance (www.elance.com)**
- **oDesk (www.odesk.com)**

Article Spinning

- **The Best Spinner (www.thebestspinner.com)**

If choosing to use this tool, adequate caution is advised. The Best Spinner will replace content within your article with synonyms to create multiple unique articles, essentially changing the wording of your content.

Chapter 7

I Spy a Competitive Advantage

When it comes to competing on the web, information about websites ranking in the position you are attempting to reach is tremendously useful. If you want to attain a certain rank for a specific search term, it stands to reason that the best plan of action is to replicate the strategies of websites that have already reached the position you're after. Therefore, it makes sense to better understand what a website is doing to achieve its success.

In Chapter 2, SpyFu was mentioned as a powerful tool to research search terms. This tool can also be used to research the top organic searches driving traffic to competitor websites. Better yet, a lot of this information is available for free, without even signing up for a paid account.

Simply go to SpyFu (**www.spyfu.com**) and type in the name of a competitor's website you want to investigate. For example, if I wanted to review the website **www.cars.com**, I would get a list of this particular site's top organic keywords and top organic competitors:

Organic Keywords		Top Organic Competitors
Rank	Term	Domain
1	2001 dodge neon	edmunds.com
1	2001 gmc sierra	autotrader.com
2	1989 honda accord	everycarlisted.com
2	1991 acura integra	motortrend.com
2	1992 ford explorer	thecarconnection.com
2	1992 honda accord	kbb.com
2	1992 honda civic	automobilemag.com

Keep in mind that I'm focusing specifically on organic keywords and competitors since that is my primary focus in increasing overall website traffic and sales. However, SpyFu will also provide details around paid marketing as well if that's a focus I were interested in pursuing.

As you can see from this chart, this research provides a handful of search terms that account for quite a bit of search volume on the site in question, as well as a handful of organic competitors. If you signed up for a paid account (even for a month), you would have access to a substantially larger amount of searches and competitors available in the SpyFu database. However, for our purposes, this should provide a great start for reviewing the competition.

If a competitor website appears to be doing well in the search rankings, it stands to reason that the site owner put some effort into their search engine presence. If you were able to identify the specific search terms that your competitor is using, you would be able to benefit from the hard work that competitor has already done to identify target search terms that will increase search engine traffic.

If you recall in Chapter 3, I advised against using meta keywords on your website because it can give away competitive intelligence about your SEO priorities. If you simply right-click on a competitor's site, you can view their source code:

Then just look for the meta keyword tags and you'll see which keywords are being targeted by the specific website.

Competitive Link Building

I cannot stress enough the impact a strong link profile will have on your search engine rankings. Getting other sites to link back to you is the best way to prove to the search engines that you are producing information and content that matters to their searchers.

In that regard, there are tools at our disposal that actually identify links being received by websites ranking for the search terms we're targeting. Can you see the opportunity this presents?

It stands to reason that if certain sites have chosen to link to websites similar to yours, these sites might also be willing to link to your site. For this purpose, we're going to do a little research and spy on the competition, so to speak.

For competitive link building, there are quite a few great tools out there that can provide tremendous value by helping to identify link-building opportunities.

With this in mind, here are some of the biggest tools out there that can help with these types of activities:

- Moz ($99/month and offers free trial)
http://www.moz.com

  Moz provides tools to help optimize local business listings, track social media performance, conduct link research, access SEO metrics and much more.

- Raven Tools ($99/month and offers free trial)
http://raventools.com

  Raven Tools utilizes data from multiple sources, including Moz, to offer a powerful suite of tools to help you research and manage link-building opportunities.

- Majestic SEO ($49.99/month and offers free trial)
https://www.majesticseo.com

  Majestic SEO is a powerful source of link information that can allow you to see the link profiles and incoming links being received by nearly any site.

- WebCEO ($49/month and offers free trial)

http://www.webceo.com

WebCEO offers a suite of tools for nearly every SEO activity imaginable. Some of the more useful tools include a content submission service, backlink manager, website auditor, and a rank checker.

- Buzz Stream (starts at $19/month and offers free trial) **http://www.buzzstream.com**

  Buzz Stream was specifically constructed with link building in mind. It is designed to automate the link-building process as much as possible, thereby minimizing the time commitment. Some of the more popular features include a research tool to help find prioritized linking opportunities, outreach assistance to help you seamlessly reach out to potential link partners, and detailed tracking and reporting so you can identify how these efforts are paying off.

As an example of competitive link building, you can go to **www.moz.com** to use their Open Site Explorer tool under the Research Tools section. Just enter the URL of one of your competitors into the toolbar to find out who is linking to their website. This tool is free to use and can provide some great information about potential linking opportunities.

Moz will provide you with a list of sites linking to whatever website you put into their tool, which you can then download into an Excel spreadsheet for your records.

Once you download the Excel report, you'll be able to view websites that are linking to your competition and would therefore potentially be willing to link to your site as well.

Now that you have a list of sites that may be interested in linking to you, it's time to reach out to the site owners and make your request. In order to do this, you'll need to find an administrative contact for the website, so I'd like to share a secret for a very effective way to find most website owners. Simply go to **http://www.whois.com/whois/** and type in the website you're trying to contact. WHOIS is a great resource that provides contact details for just about every website, as long as it hasn't been privately registered. This can definitely be an invaluable resource when attempting to do outreach for link-building purposes.

Here's a typical e-mail I use to ask for a link from the site owner:

Hi,

I came across your site when doing a Google search and was really impressed. I actually represent a site that (list what your business does here). Therefore, I was hoping you'd consider including it as a resource for your audience as well. The website is nameofsite.com, and I think your audience will find it to be very useful. If you need any further details, I'd be happy to provide them to you. Please just let me know, and thanks for your time.

Regards,

Your Name

In this regard, Buzz Stream (which is mentioned earlier in this chapter) can be a great tool to help automate some of your link outreach efforts. If you don't ask for a link, you won't get a link. I'll warn you that this process can be fairly tedious, and the response rate will vary depending on the type of business you're in and how competitive it is. Keep those expectations in mind. The quality of the links can be strong, but the process can be limiting based on how manual and tedious this type of outreach tends to be. I recommend reaching out to the websites that have the best potential for you to acquire links in order to make the most efficient use of your time.

At this point, I would like to state again that while there is extensive detail provided in this book about how to leverage the tools of Moz to effectively execute various SEO tactics, this is not the only resource out there. I've focused on Moz specifically because the tools provided by this company have emerged as some of the best and most respected in the SEO space to date. Furthermore, Moz is an all-inclusive resource to assist with nearly every aspect related to search engine optimization.

With that being said, the world of SEO is very fluid and constantly evolving. Therefore, the strategies outlined in this chapter and others have been designed to show you how to effectively use these resources for the purpose of getting more website traffic. Moz is in no way the only provider offering these kinds of tools to help manage an effective SEO campaign. My goal is to provide you with specific examples and knowledge of how these tools work so you can then use these and similar tools to create the results you want. So feel free to experiment with the various tools that are outlined in this book so that you can find the resources that work best for your personal working style and goals.

With these resources at your disposal, it's only a matter of getting familiarized with the techniques. Once you do that, you'll be a link-acquiring machine. You'll have a huge advantage over the competition, increasing both your search rankings and relevance for the terms for which you are attempting to rank. The increase in links you acquire will be a huge driver in improving your search rankings.

Let's see your competitors keep up with you when you apply all of these newfound strategies!

- **SEO Challenge #5: Link Outreach**
  Look up the Meta keywords for your top 3 competitors. How many keywords were you able to find that weren't in your initial list of targeted search terms?

- **Tools And Tricks**

SEO Research Tools

- **SpyFu (www.spyfu.com)**

Research competitors and find the search terms that are driving the most traffic to their websites on a monthly basis.

SEO Software Tools

- **Moz (www.moz.com)**

Moz offers a complete set of software, tools, and resources to maximize your search engine optimization. Paid members get access to their campaign-based web application, dozens of SEO tools, webinars, and full access to Open Site Explorer, a powerful resource for researching competitor link profiles.

- **Raven Tools (www.raventools.com)**

Raven Tools utilizes data from multiple sources, including Moz, to offer a powerful suite of tools to help you research and manage link-building opportunities. These tools are designed to help you with a range of functions, such as managing your campaign, building links, checking ranks, conducting competitive analysis, and monitoring your social media channels.

- **Majestic SEO (www.majesticseo.com)**

Majestic SEO is a powerful source of link information that can allow you to see the link profiles and incoming links being received by nearly any site. For reviewing the incoming links for your site or a competitor's, this could very well be the best of the best.

- **WebCEO (www.webceo.com)**

WebCEO offers a suite of tools for nearly every SEO activity imaginable. Some of the more useful tools include a content submission service, backlink manager, website auditor, and rank checker.

- **Buzz Stream (www.buzzstream.com)**

Buzz Stream is a CRM for link building and PR/social media that allows online marketers like you manage relationships and get results, whether you are looking to increase your incoming links or gain exposure through a press release.

Website Owner Research

- **WHOIS (www.whois.com/whois)**

The WHOIS database contains information related to websites such as assignees, registrants, administrative information, and website creation and expiration dates.

Chapter 8

Getting Social Wins You Friends

Social bookmarking is a godsend for publishers of news sites, blogs, and other websites. Social bookmarking can introduce your site to new people with relevant interests and can drive site traffic and valuable incoming links. So what exactly is social bookmarking?

Have you ever found a website that you wanted to remember so you bookmarked it on your browser for easy reference?

If you're not quite sure how to do this, you can find a tutorial here: ehow.com/how_5420_bookmark-web-page.html. The process will vary a bit by Internet browser.

It's important that you understand this concept, as there are distinct similarities to social bookmarking. In fact, social bookmarking is the same as bookmarking any website in your browser. The only difference is that social bookmarks are saved on a website and not on your local computer. So it doesn't matter which computer you use, you always have your bookmarks available to you.

Let's take a look at how you actually go about social bookmarking.

Step 1) You need to register with the target social bookmarking website and get your e-mail address verified.

Step 2) Add the website to your social bookmarking account.

Step 3) Submit the appropriate information about your website into the title and description window.

After that, simply fill out the details, hit the save button, and you've successfully created a social bookmark for your site. It's a simple process that can have a profound impact on your search engine rankings.

Now that you know how the process works, here's an extensive list of sites for social bookmarking purposes. It's compiled according to Google PageRank, so go nuts and get your social bookmark on.

Page Rank	Site	Website URL
9	Yahoo! Bookmarks	www.bookmarks.yahoo.com
9	Google Bookmarks	www.google.com/bookmarks/
8	Blinklist	www.blinklist.com/index.php?Action=Blink/
8	Digg	www.digg.com/news/business
8	Slashdot	www.slashdot.org/
8	Cite U Like	www.citeulike.org/posturl

Page Rank	Site	Website URL
8	Connotea	www.connotea.org/ addpopup
8	Delicious	www.delicious.com/ login?lo_action=save&next
8	Reddit	www.ssl.reddit.com/ login?
8	Stumble Upon	www.stumbleupon.com/ signup
8	Tumblr	www.tumblr.com/register
7	Bibsonomy	www.bibsonomy.org/ register
7	Folkd	www.folkd.com/page/ register.html
7	Squidoo	www.squidoo. com/lensmaster/ bookmark?%url%
7	Diigo	secure.diigo.com/sign-up
6	Dzone	www.dzone.com/links/ index.html
6	Hotklix	www.hotklix.com/addlink
6	Kaboodle	www.kaboodle.com/
6	Kwoff	www.kwoff.com/login. php?return=/submit.php
6	Link A Go Go	www.linkagogo.com/go/ UserInfo
6	Start Aid	www.startaid.com/
5	Buddy Marks	www.buddymarks.com/ login.php
5	Design Bump	www.designbump.com/ submit

Page Rank	Site	Website URL
5	She Told Me	www.shetoldme.com/user/register
5	Tagza	www.tagza.com/login.php?return=/submit
5	Give A Link	www.givealink.org/account/new
5	Netvouz	www.netvouz.com/action/submitBookmark
5	You Mob	youmob.com/startmob.aspx
4	Blog Marks	www.blogmarks.net/my/new.php
4	Cloudy Tags	www.cloudytags.com/submit.html
4	Fwisp	www.fwisp.com/login.php?return=/submit
4	Give A Link	www.givealink.org/account/new
4	MURL	www.murl.com/newuser/
4	Qaafe	www.qaafe.com/login.php?return=/submit
4	BM Access	www.bmaccess.net/submit
4	CoRank	www.corank.com/signUp.html
4	Fark	www.fark.com/submit/
4	My HQ	www.myhq.com/cgi-bin/all/register.cgi
4	Rambhai	www.rambhai.com/register

Page Rank	Site	Website URL
4	Chipmark	www.chipmark.com/Register
4	White Links	www.whitelinks.com/whitelinks/signup.php
3	En Express	www.enexpress.net/login.php?return=/submit
3	KWZZ	www.kwzz.com/
3	My Link Vault	www.mylinkvault.com/users/register.php
3	Bookmark 4 U	www.bookmark4you.com/register
3	Gozoof	www.gozoof.com/AddLink.aspx
3	Social Bookmarking	www.social-bookmarking.net/login.php
2	Dizzed	www.dizzed.com/login.php?return=/submit.php
2	Eggig	www.eggig.com/login.php?return=/submit.php
2	Kannikar	www.kannikar.com/login.php?return=/submit
2	Link Submit	www.linksubmitz.com/register/
2	My Tidbits	www.mytitbits.com/login.php?return=/submit.php
2	SAEO	www.saeo.net/login.php?return=/submit

Page Rank	Site	Website URL
2	Wall Paper Joint	www.wallpaperjoint.com/login.php?return=/submit
2	Book Mark All	www.bookmarkall.com/bookmark/default.aspx
2	Zeegal	www.zeegal.com/login.php?return=/submit
1	Kojaxx	www.kojaxx.com/login.php?return=/submit
1	Blurpalicious	www.blurpalicious.com/login.php?return=/submit
1	Link Roll	www.linkroll.com/index.php?action=registration

When prioritizing your social bookmarking efforts, it's important to note that, as mentioned earlier, PageRank is a value that Google places on a website in terms of the level of importance that it has given to a particular website. PageRank values will fluctuate between one and ten, with ten being the highest rating possible. Therefore, the higher the PageRank, the more importance Google places on the link being given out by the website.

Social bookmarking is just one part of the social strategy involved in winning on the web. These days, utilizing Facebook, Twitter, and even Google Plus for your business can help you better engage with your audience and build a strong link profile in the process. While social media still has a somewhat minimal impact on SEO in terms of factors being considered by Google's algorithms, that impact is growing all the time, and Google has indicated that it will play a more prevalent part in their rankings in the near future. Also, leveraging social media is a great way to get your content shared so that you naturally build your incoming links. Therefore, you should be aware of some opportunities and tools to help you manage your social media presence.

If you haven't already, you should definitely sign up for a Facebook business page for your website. Simply go here to set up a page for your business: **https://www.facebook.com/business/build.** Once your page is created, you will want to invite friends, customers, and colleagues to become a fan of your new Facebook business page. Next, you will want to post quality messages on your page that serve to engage your audience. Also, encourage fans to publicize your information to their friends by offering interesting information, contests, or other incentives that will drive your audience to share your page. This is a great opportunity to engage your audience and drive incoming links in the process.

Another highly regarded tool for SEO purposes is Twitter. You can learn more about setting up a Twitter account for your business here: https://business.twitter.com/. Twitter can be a great tool to help you stay involved in the conversation and encourage incoming links. One tool that will help you to find Twitter users interested in your business is **www.tweetadder.com.** For $55, you can open an account and look for people following topics related to your site. Then you can simply add them, and they will add you in return. This is a great way to get people to follow your Twitter account if they are interested in what your site has to offer. By sharing with them, they can then pass your messages on, and this can help you generate incoming links.

Once you've set up your Facebook and Twitter accounts, a great tool to help schedule posts and monitor these accounts is Hoot Suite (**www.hootsuite.com**). Hoot Suite offers a free or paid account; you can initially get set up with the free version for these purposes.

A more recent social media platform that has burst onto the scene in a big way is Google Plus. One big advantage of Google Plus is that the largest search engine in the world created it. This gives the platform instant credibility. With any social media platform, the usefulness of the network is tied closely to the number of active users the network is able to attract. In this regard, Google Plus has surpassed five hundred million active users. This is an impressive feat for such a young platform. In quite a few ways, Google Plus closely resembles Facebook. To create a business Google Plus page, you set it up here: **www.google.com/+/business**. Then, similarly to Facebook, you will want to invite friends, customers, and colleagues to click on the plus-one button Google will create for you so you can create groups in your Google Plus account. This is also known as Google Circles and is very similar to the process of liking a page on Facebook. The one big difference between Google Plus and Facebook is that with Google Plus you have the ability to categorize your sharing, so you can share different content with different groups of people depending on how you've categorized them. This is a great feature for content sharing through social media.

While Google Plus is still fairly new, it appears Google will be integrating more heavily into some of its searches the social signals it collects from Google Plus. Since Google owns this platform, it will be easier for them to measure the social signals they extract. Also, it will be easier for Google to tweak Google Plus to get the types of social signals they deem important for their search rankings. Furthermore, Google has been trying to become a major factor in social media since 2004 and will be heavily invested in making Google Plus a success. There has already been some testing regarding the effects of building a Google Plus following on increased search engine rankings, and there appears to be a correlation between the two. When it comes to SEO tactics, you want every advantage for ranking on the search engines. Therefore, I highly recommended you implement the Google Plus One button on your website and encourage your audience to join your Google Plus circle, since this could very well be something that is heavily integrated into future searches. Getting a jump on this now could provide a tremendous competitive advantage.

There's one other thing I would like to discuss regarding social media. In terms of your ability to drive awareness, gain incoming links, and use this to your advantage to increase search engine rankings, the size of your audience is very important. If you only have a few followers on Twitter, a couple of fans on Facebook, and no one signed up on your Google circles, social media won't do much for your online ambitions. There is a tool, though, that can be very helpful in expanding your social reach and driving the natural sharing of your content, which is very important in the online world. If you're interested in experimenting with social media sharing, sign up for a trial account at TribePro (**www.tribepro.com**). There, you'll have the ability to join niche groups where you share out members' content with your followers and they reciprocate in kind. This can be a powerful way to spread your content without having to rely solely on the community you have built. So feel free to give it a try and do your best to get your content to go viral. You'll be very surprised at what you can accomplish.

While it can take a while to build a stellar backlink profile relying on social media sites, they do have some influence over search engine rankings and are growing in importance all the time. So get social and win friends, because link building really is like a popularity contest.

- **SEO Challenge #6: Social Bookmarking**
  Sign up for an account at Delicious.com and get your website bookmarked on the site. How long did it take you to complete this process?

- **Tools And Tricks**

Social Media for Business

- **Facebook (www.facebook.com/business/build)**

While everyone knows about Facebook these days, it is still significantly underutilized by businesses. With a strong Facebook presence, you will be able to build relationships with your customers, reach new people, and drive sales. Over one billion people like and comment an average of 3.2 billion times every day on Facebook. When you have a strong Facebook presence, your business is part of these conversations and has access to the most powerful kind of word-of-mouth marketing—***recommendations between friends***. Furthermore, Facebook can be great for getting information shared virally while increasing your incoming links at the same time.

- **Twitter (https://business.twitter.com)**

While Twitter is a well-known social tool, most businesses don't realize how invaluable this resource can be for engaging with current and prospective customers. Twitter is an information network that brings people closer to what's important to them. Every day, millions of people turn to Twitter to connect about their interests, share information, and find out what's happening in the world. I highly recommend that any business looking to increase their customer base take full advantage of this vast communication network.

- **Google Plus (http://www.google.com/+/business)**

Although Google Plus is fairly new to the social media world, it is owned by Google and starting to demonstrate some heavy influence on how social signals impact everyday searches. With over five hundred million active users and the ability to set up specific categories for your followers with Google Circles, this platform is quickly becoming a necessity for any business looking to gain an advantage in increasing search engine rankings and overall awareness.

Social Media Management

- **Tweet Adder (www.tweetadder.com)**

Tweet Adder is a powerful tool to effectively build a community of Twitter followers interested in your topics of choice. You can open an account and look for people following topics related to your website. Add them, and they will add you in return. This is a great way to engage with people interested in what your site offers. You share with them, and they then pass your messages on, helping you generate incoming links as well as interest in your business or website.

- **Hoot Suite (www.hootsuite.com)**

Hoot Suite is a premier social media tool that helps manage and measure the biggest social media networks, such as Facebook, Twitter, and LinkedIn. In a complex social world, a tool such as Hoot Suite can be invaluable for keeping track of your online social presence and scheduling messages through your social media accounts.

Social Media .Content Distribution

- **Tribe Pro (www.tribepro.com)**

Tribe Pro is an innovative content syndication platform for social media. This resource will help you find a community of bloggers, social networks, and online marketers who are helping each other to succeed on the Internet by bookmarking and sharing each other's content across various social media outlets. There is no better way to build up your social profile than to connect with a like-minded group of online marketers who are willing and able to reach out to the very audience you are seeking to attract.

Chapter 9

Directory Submit, Rinse, Repeat

During the early days of the Internet, directory submissions used to play a substantial role in search engine rankings. In today's more complex world, search engines have gotten much more sophisticated in the way they determine rankings. That being said, there is still some value to submitting your website to directories.

The goal with this chapter is to help you identify how to find directories that will have the greatest impact on your link-building efforts and how to do so without paying a dime to the directories for inclusion. So let's cut through the clutter, save time, and focus on directory submissions only where and when it makes sense.

It's important to be very careful when submitting your site to directories. The practice of obtaining links from online directories has changed dramatically over the past few years. Poor-quality, spam-induced directories currently flood the Internet, and an unfocused effort to obtain links from these all-inclusive directories can actually harm your SEO efforts. Therefore, it's more important than ever to have an evolved and focused strategy when engaging in directory submissions.

Let's begin with what directory submissions are and how they can positively impact your search engine rankings. The concept is actually quite simple. You find a directory, such as **www.botw.org**, you select a category relevant to your site, and you then list your website info. The profile typically consists of the site's title, a short description, any relevant key search terms, and the site's web address. Once you fill out your information, you hit submit and you're up on the directory once approved. Sounds simple enough, right?

Unfortunately, like so many things in life, it's a bit more complicated than it appears on the surface.

First, there's the process of finding directories and manually submitting requests to each one over and over again. There are bulk services out there that offer to do this for a nominal fee. Most of them are complete scams, though. Stay away from them and the information in this book has already paid for itself.

Second, there are always multiple options with these directories. Typically, the options involve paying for a link, adding a link on your own site in exchange for receiving a link, or submitting a regular link without the above requirements. Would you ever pay or add a link on your site if you didn't have to? Probably not. Often, the directory threatens to take up to six months to get you listed, if they even allow it at all, unless you offer to pay for inclusion or include a link on your website that points back to the directory. Don't worry about that.

My advice is to never add a link to your site or pay for inclusion; the benefit is almost never worth the cost. The best-quality directories provide free links because it encourages more businesses to register, which in turn makes their directories more useful. Also, adding a link to your site could actually harm your SEO efforts, as Google penalizes sites that are viewed as having lists of links with no relevant value.

So now that you've been thoroughly frightened with the potential perils of directories, let's dive into the process and discuss some things to look out for.

Anyone interested in increasing his or her business or entity's online presence should consider actively submitting to some directories with a high page ranking.

In this book you will find a list of two hundred *free* directories to which you can submit your site. I would recommend starting with the highest-valued directories in terms of page rank and then moving down the list. All of these directories should offer the opportunity to submit your site for free, but be aware that your site may take some time to show up and get placement.

Before going too crazy with the directories listed below, I'd like to add a word of caution about directory submissions. Recently, Google has begun penalizing sites deemed "over-optimized." What this means is that if your site appears to have tremendous amounts of directories pointing back to it for no other reason than receiving a link, it could harm your efforts. Therefore, I strongly recommend you submit to ten or so on this list, review your progress for a month, and then submit some more. Slow and steady can definitely help you win this race.

With that being said, here is a list of two hundred *free* directories:

Page Rank	Site	Website URL
8	DMOZ	www.dmoz.org/docs/en/add.html
8	Yahoo Directory	www.ecom.yahoo.com/dir/submit/
8	Business.com	www.secure.business.com/crm/signup/
6	Hitmaroc	www.hitmaroc.net/submit.php
6	ABC Directory	www.abc-directory.com/submiturl
6	Elib	www.elib.org/how_add.php
6	Ezilon	www.ezilon.com/general_url_submission.htm
6	Free PR Web Directory	www.freeprwebdirectory.com/submit.php
6	Haaba	www.haabaa.com/add-your-site.html
6	Joe Ant	www.joeant.com/suggest.html
6	Qango	www.qango.com/addurl.html
6	Scrub The Web	www.scrubtheweb.com/addurl.html

Page Rank	Site	Website URL
5	A Big Directory	www.abigdir.com/submit.php
5	Adler Directory	www.adlerspace.com/submit.php
5	Apali	www.apali.com/apalicgi/afegir-urlEN.asp
5	Baikal Global	www.baikalglobal.com/submit.php
5	Link Centre	www.linkcentre.com/addurl/
5	The Little Web Directory	www.littlewebdirectory.com/links.asp
5	Official Search	www.officialsearch.com/submit.html
5	One Mission	www.onemission.com/mail.pl
5	RCR Education	www.rcreducation.com/submit.php
5	So Much	www.somuch.com/AddSite/
5	APEX	www.a-p-e-x.org/submit.php
5	All The Biz	www.allthebizz.com/how_add.php
5	Arakne Links	www.arakne-links.com/submit.php

Page Rank	Site	Website URL
5	Aviva Directory	www.avivadirectory.com/submit.php
5	Busy Bits	www.busybits.com/files/add.php
5	Cyber Web Search	www.cyberwebsearch.com/
5	Illumirate	www.illumirate.com/add_your_site_exp.cfm
5	Info Tiger	www.infotiger.com/addurl.html
5	Link And Think	www.linkandthink.org/submit.php
5	Re-Quest	www.re-quest.net/add-url.htm
5	Smaller Biz Directories	www.smallerbizz.com/how_add.php
5	So Much	www.somuch.com/AddSite/SubmitMain.asp
5	Submit.biz	www.submit.biz/
5	Surf Safely	www.surfsafely.com/urladd.html
5	T Section	www.tsection.com/content/add/
5	Web World Index	www.webworldindex.com/submit.htm
5	World Site Index	www.worldsiteindex.com/index.php
5	Zen Search	www.zensearch.com/submit.shtml

Page Rank	Site	Website URL
5	Zepti	www.zepti.net/addsite.html
4	9 Sites	www.9sites.net/addurl.php
4	A Flat	www.a-flat.org/submit.php
4	Add A 4U	www.adda4u.com/submit.php
4	Submit Free	www.addsite-submit-free.com/submit.php
4	Aedpws	www.aedpws.org/submit.php
4	Ajooja	www.ajooja.com/cgi-bin/user.cgi
4	Alarmg 4s	www.alarmg4s.com/submit.php
4	A List Directory	www.alistdirectory.com/submit.php
4	Better SEO Directory	www.betterseodirectory.com/submit.php
4	Beverly FM	www.beverlyfm.com/submit.php
4	Black Absolute	www.blackabsolute.com/submit.php
4	Blavagen	www.blavagen.com/submit.php
4	Bull Dog Blog	www.bulldogblog.net/submit.php
4	Bullogs Directory	www.bullogs.com/submit.php

Page Rank	Site	Website URL
4	Caboose Open Directory	www.cabooseopendirectory.com/addurl.php
4	Colorado SPH	www.coloradosph.org/submit.php
4	Counter Deal	www.counterdeal.com/submit.php
4	Ctap 7	www.ctap7.org/submit.php
4	Drop Clear Directory	www.dropclear.com/submit.php
4	E Whose Directory	www.ewhose.com/submit.php
4	Extreme Green Directory	www.extreme-green.net/submit.php
4	Fat 64	www.fat64.net/submit.php
4	Hdrtvu	www.hdrtvu.org/submit.php
4	Hydra Web	www.hydraweb.com/submit.php
4	i25 Business Directory	www.i25northforty.com/submit.php
4	Ithaca Forward	www.ithacaforward.org/submit.php
4	Kitchenaid Plaza	www.kitchenaidplaza.com/submit.php

Page Rank	Site	Website URL
4	Linkroo	www.linkroo.com/submit.php
4	Magdalyns	www.magdalyns.com/submit.php
4	Minkees Directory	www.minkees.com/submit.php
4	Net Insert	www.netinsert.com/en/insert.html
4	NI Resource	www.niresource.com/submit.php
4	Nits Bizarcade	www.nits-bizarcade.com/submit.php
4	Ogden Score	www.ogdenscore.com/submit.php
4	Reality Radio	www.realityradio1320.com/submit.php
4	Review USA Directory	www.revusa.com/submit.php
4	Search Site	www.searchsight.com/submit.htm
4	Sladco	www.sladco.com/submit.php
4	Smart Links	www.smartlinks.us/submit.php
4	Snap CC	www.snapcc.org/submit.php

Page Rank	Site	Website URL
4	TCAD International	www.tcad-international.com/submit.php
4	TFSN	www.tfsn.org/submit.php
4	The Net Directory	www.the-net-directory.com/submit.php
4	The Great Directory	www.thegreatdirectory.org/submit.php
4	The Need Info	www.theneedinfo.com/submit%20link.html
4	The SEO King	www.theseoking.com/submit.php
4	Txt Links	www.txtlinks.com/sug_url.php
4	Urng Maiz	www.urng-maiz.com/submit.php
4	Vie Search	www.viesearch.com/submit
4	Aardvark Business	www.aardvarkbusiness.net/addurl/
4	All Business Directory	www.allbusinessdirectory.biz/directory.php
4	Amray	www.amray.com/add_url_instructions.html
4	Ask Matrix	www.askmatrix.com/submit/
4	Best Free Websites	www.bestfreewebsites.net/suggest-listing.php

Page Rank	Site	Website URL
4	Business Seek	www.businessseek.biz/link_submit.php
4	Buy SLL	www.buysll.com/sub-mit.php
4	Cipinet	www.cipinet.com/sub-mit.php
4	Claymont	www.claymont.com/submitnologin.asp
4	Clickey	www.clickey.com/signup.shtml
4	Cluboo	www.cluboo.com/sub-mit.php
4	Code 3 Directory	www.code3directory.com/submit.php
4	Code Classic	www.codeclassic.net/submit.php
4	Director Am	www.directory.am/add.php
4	LDM Studio	www.directory.ldmstu-dio.com/add/add.php
4	Domaining In	www.domaining.in/sub-mit.php
4	Earth Station 9	www.earthstation9.com/
4	Free Directory Submit	www.freedirectorysub-mit.com/submit.php
4	Fresh TV	www.freshtv.com/sub-mit.php
4	Gain Web	www.gainweb.org/sub-mit.php

Page Rank	Site	Website URL
4	H&R Enterprises	www.hrent.com/add_link.html
4	Info Listings	www.info-listings.com/submit.php
4	Link Add URL	www.linkaddurl.com/submit.php
4	Link Teve	www.linkteve.com/submit.php
4	Marketing Internet Directory	www.marketinginternetdirectory.com
4	Pro Link Directory	www.prolinkdirectory.com/submit.php
4	Qazee	www.qazee.com/directory/submit.php
4	Search The Web	www.searchtheweb.com/suggest/
4	SEO Directory	www.seodirectoryonline.org/SubmitLink/
4	Site Promotion Directory	www.sitepromotiondirectory.com/submit.php
4	Sites Plus	www.sites-plus.com/submit.php
4	Skaffe	www.skaffe.com/info/addurl.php
4	Starting Point Directory	www.stpt.com/directory/addsite.htm

Page Rank	Site	Website URL
4	Submission 4 U	www.submission4u.com/submit.php
4	Vox Cap	www.voxcap.com/submit.php
4	Website Services	www.website-services.biz/submit.php
4	Wikid Web	www.wikid-web.com/wiki/Help:Add_an_entry
4	Yeandi	www.yeandi.com/addurl.asp
4	Zim Engine	www.zimengine.com/submit.php
3	4 WHPL	www.4wh.pl/add.php
3	7 Si	www.7si.org/submit.php
3	AAA Web Directory	www.aaawebdirectory.com/submit.php
3	Add 2 Directory	www.add2dir.info/submit.php
3	Add Site Free	www.addsitefree.com/submit.php
3	Arbecey Directory	www.arbecey.com/submit.php
3	BP Directory	www.bpdir.com/submit.php

Page Rank	Site	Website URL
3	Business Finder	www.business-finder.info/submit.php
3	CCWOS	www.ccwos.com/submit.php
3	Chaqra	www.chaqra.com/submit.php
3	Cyan Directory	www.cyandir.com/submit.php
3	DHD Photo	www.dhdphoto.com/submit.php
3	Campus TI	www.directory.campusti.org/submit.html
3	Soveb Directory	www.directory.soveb.org/submit.html
3	Directory Wind	www.directorywind.com/submit.php
3	Facility Reporting	www.facilityreporting.org/submit.php
3	Great Directory	www.ggfb.org/submit.php
3	Joint MC	www.jointmc.com/submit.php
3	JSUM Directory	www.jsum.org/submit.php
3	List Your Website	www.list-your-website.com/submit.php

Page Rank	Site	Website URL
3	Montello Fish Fun	www.montellofishnfun.com/submit.php
3	Nuclear Land	www.nuclearland.com/submit.php
3	Ofcourse Directory	www.ofcourse.us/add.php
3	Place Your Links	www.placeyourlinks.com/submit.php
3	PR3 Plus	www.pr3plus.com/submit.php
3	Quick Directory	www.quickdirectory.biz/index.php?ms=4
3	Sonicrun	www.search.sonicrun.com/sitesubmission
3	Site Listings	www.sitelistings.net/submit.php
3	Stonever	www.stonever.com/add.php
3	Submit 2 Directory	www.submit2dir.info/submit.php
3	Submit Link	www.submitlink.info/submit.php
3	Web O World	www.weboworld.com/free_form.php
3	WMSW	www.wmsw.org/submit.php

Page Rank	Site	Website URL
3	Wondex	www.wondex.com/submit.php
3	Add Page	www.add-page.com/siteadd/add_0_0.php
3	All The Websites	www.allthewebsites.org/login.php
3	Ask Directory	www.askdirectory.com/cgi-bin/addurl.cgi
3	Best Websites	www.best-websites.net/Create-new-item
3	Bys	www.bys.net/link_submit_option.php
3	Clubs Page	www.clubspage.net/Addurl/index.html
3	Directory Free	www.directory-free.com/submit/submit.php
3	Directory Sphere	www.directorysphere.com/index.php
3	Dramba	www.dramba.com/index php?location=link_add
3	Exact Seek	www.exactseek.com/add.html
3	Featured Blahoo	www.featured.blahoo.net/submit.php

Page Rank	Site	Website URL
3	Free Website Directory	www.freewebsitedirectory.com/submit.php
3	G Dotz	www.gdotz.com/submit.php
3	Good Directory	www.gooddirectory.net/index.php
3	I Do Find	www.idofind.com/addurl/index.html
3	Infignos	www.infignos.com/addlisting/speedlist.cfm
3	Itz A List	www.itzalist.com/url-submission.html
3	Jayde	www.jayde.com/submit.html
3	Jewana	www.jewana.com/submit.php
3	Link Dir 4 U	www.linkdir4u.com/submit-link.php
3	Links Pub	www.linkspub.com/submit-site.phtml
3	Mavicanet	www.mavicanet.com/
3	Pegasus Directory	www.pegasusdirectory.com/submit.php
3	Powerfull Directory	www.powerfulldirectory.info/submit.php

Page Rank	Site	Website URL
3	Search 24	www.searchtwentyfour.com/Templates/index.php
3	Seo Target	www.seotarget.net/submit.php
3	Sgt Search	www.sgtsearch.com/submit/
3	Skype Media	www.skypemedia.com/submit.php
3	Suggest URL	www.suggest-url.net/suggest-url.php
3	Umoz Directory	www.umoz.org/submit/
3	UU Directory	www.uudir.com/Submit.aspx
3	Web Central	www.web-central.info/AddSite.aspx
3	Websquash	www.websquash.com/cgi-bin/dir/add.cgi
3	Web To Tell	www.webtotell.com/suggest-listing.php
3	Xland	www.xland.info/sub-mit.php
3	Zunch Directory	www.zunchdirectory.com/SubmissionGuide.aspx
3	Zenome	www.zenome.com/indexing/index.php

Now that we have a large list of directories to which we can submit our website, let's walk through how this process will look.

With most major directories, there's an option to submit a link, submit a site, register a company, or some variation thereof.

Once you do this, you'll typically be given instructions on the submission process and requirements. For example, on DMOZ you're instructed to go to the home page, select the single best category for your website, and then hit the Suggest URL link once you've reached the category you believe is most appropriate.

After you click Suggest URL, you'll have the opportunity to give details on the business itself, which will serve as your listing in the directory listing being set up.

Simply input your e-mail and you're good to go.

Make sure that you mention your main services and products when creating your description. This is similar to the descriptions you used on the local map citations earlier.

Now just repeat a few dozen times and you'll have mastered the directories to increase your search engine rankings.

> **SEO Challenge #7: Directory Submissions**
> Submit your website to both DMOZ and the Yahoo! Directory. Did you have any trouble finding the right category when submitting?

Chapter 10

Getting Blogged Down

Blogging can help your SEO efforts in a few different ways. When you blog, you're creating unique content that will help the search engines identify your site as an authoritative resource on your subject matter. And when you contribute to other blogs and forums, it can help you build up your link profile.

I highly recommend that you have your own blog. The two biggest players out there, the services that by far facilitate the most blogs for the biggest bloggers, are WordPress (**www.wordpress.com**) and Blogger (**www.blogger.com**). The good news is that both of these services provide options that are free or very inexpensive, and both are extremely easy to use. If you want a blog as part of your website, I strongly encourage you to go to WordPress or Blogger and set one up.

When you sign up with these services, you will be offered a free option hosted and supported by the service you choose or an inexpensive option that allows you to set up the blog on any domain that you want to use. If you are serious about getting into blogging, I highly recommend you set up the blog on your own domain. Once you start to amass traffic and an audience, it will be very difficult to flip a switch and transfer all that you have built to your own domain down the line. It is completely up to you, based on how much blogging you think you will actually do, but using your own domain name is definitely the preferred way to go if you plan on making blogging a significant component of your online presence.

Once your blog is set up and ready to go, you will need to create content for it. Update your blog at least once or twice a week. No need to overdo it, but you should definitely keep your blog active.

When it comes to blogging, the bottom line is that you'd better like to write—or work with someone who does. If you don't have the time or ability to maintain a steady flow of blog content, try to make time. It can pay off substantially.

If you want to hire a company to help with this writing, you can always contract an outside vendor to help or use some of the same companies listed in Chapter 6:

- **www.elance.com**
- **www.odesk.com**
- **www.iwriter.com**
- **www.99centarticles.com**
- **www.articleninjas.com**
- **www.articlesontap.com**
- **www.ccarticles.com**
- **www.myarticleexpress.com**

As mentioned earlier, the quality of these article-writing services and vendors can vary greatly. Depending on your industry, this can make a big difference. If you work in a complex field such as finance or law, it would be advisable to write all of the content yourself. However, these writing services are typically very inexpensive, so you really won't risk much by testing them out to see if they can write content that meets your standards.

One thing that can be said about these services—if they weren't needed, they wouldn't exist. There's obviously a glaring demand for assistance with this type of writing, which is why so many of these services are able to survive.

If you find that none of the content produced can match your finely tuned professional abilities, then I encourage you to spend a few hours a week writing strong content for your own purposes. You're going to need quite a bit of content to properly market your site, whether you post the material on your own site, contribute content as a guest blogger, distribute your postings across article sites, or use your writings to answer questions on forums. There's quite a bit of thought and effort that goes into content creation, but the payoff can be huge.

It's important to keep two things in mind when generating material. Don't continually repost the same blog entry. The search engines pick up on these activities. Also, don't create spammy articles, poorly written pieces with little value that overuse the intended keywords. If a reader would come away from your post with little to no value or added insight, then it probably shouldn't be written.

Now that we've explored how to set up a blog and various options to create the content needed, let's focus on how we can leverage these tools for our purposes.

First, use your material for internal linking. Within your own website's blog, if an article mentions a topic or service that exists elsewhere on your site, make sure the article links to the page in question.

Next, constantly create new content; one to two new articles a week, optimally. Your posts don't have to be incredibly long-winded, but they should center on topics specifically related to the search terms you are targeting. This is extremely important to keep in mind as you develop your content.

As mentioned in Chapter 6, link building is an instrumental part of article writing. Apply anchor text—wording that provides a link back to your site—for appropriate keywords to get a decent ranking.

As a reminder, anchor text is the visible characters and words that create a hyperlink display when linking to another document or location on the web. Search engines use this text to help determine the subject matter of the linked-to document.

This is such an important part of link building that I'd like to cover it again (even though it was mentioned in an earlier chapter). Here is the HTML code that would be used to properly insert an anchor text link:

<a href="**http://www.sovomedia.com**">**Seattle SEO Agency**</a>

By using this HTML code, the term "Seattle SEO Agency" can be placed in a blog or article as a text link with the link pointing to the website URL: **http://www.sovomedia.com.** This serves to inform the search engines about the subject matter of the article while building a stronger link profile and more credibility online at the same time.

When it comes to blogging, the benefits experienced from increased exposure and incoming links will be closely aligned with the size of the audience actually reading the blog. Hence, it's imperative that a good amount of effort is placed on building up a following. Having a large readership will not only help with the overall goals of SEO but will also serve as a great motivator to diligently update your blog, as you will not want to disappoint all those loyal readers.

In this regard, Triberr (**www.triberr.com**) is a great tool to help you increase your overall audience by leveraging the networks of other prominent bloggers. Triberr groups people into niches or "tribes." Every time one of the tribe members makes a blog post, a tweet is sent by all of the other tribe members to inform their blog audiences. This extended reach can be instrumental in helping small- and medium-sized bloggers band together and share each other's audience. If you recall from Chapter 8, I recommended a tool to help increase Twitter followers called Tweet Adder (**www.tweetadder.com**). Using this tool to build up your Twitter following, you will increase your ability to join some great tribes to help you promote content you post to your blog.

It's important to note that Triberr will not allow any random person to sign up. First, you have to be accepted into an existing tribe. Either you search tribes and request entry into the tribe, or you receive an invitation from an existing tribe chief. You can search based upon categories to find a tribe that is a fit for you.

Therefore, the more Twitter followers you have acquired, the higher the probability that you will be accepted into the best tribes with the biggest reach.

Another great opportunity when it comes to blogging is to write guest posts for relevant blogs. To identify high-value sites for contributing content, you can use resources that connect bloggers with potential blogs, such as Blogger Link Up (**www.bloggerlinkup.com**). Here, you can get on a free e-mail list where people post requests for blog contributions. Another reputable resource is My Blog Guest (**http://myblogguest.com**). This site will also put you in touch with respected bloggers who regularly need content related to specific areas of interest. If you write something, they'll give you a link back, which will help with your link profile.

Before going to the effort of contributing to other websites, always be sure to check out the site and its traffic statistics. You can use a tool like Alexa (**www.alexa.com**) to find relevant traffic information.

For those not familiar with Alexa, it's a great tool. The Alexa Rank is a statistic used to evaluate traffic volumes of websites. Alexa ranks the top hundred thousand websites on the Internet in terms of popularity. Alexa computes traffic rankings by analyzing the web usage of millions of Alexa users. It's basically like the Nielsen ratings of the Internet. The lower the number, the more traffic a website receives. For example, Google has a ranking of one according to Alexa, meaning that it receives the most Internet traffic out of any website in existence.

Another great opportunity to spread your content involves blogging on Web 2.0 sites. A Web 2.0 site is essentially a website that allows users to interact and collaborate with each other as creators of user-generated content in a community environment. This stands in contrast to the typical website, encouraging passive viewing of content by its users. Thus, the name Web 2.0 was created to label this new breed of interactive website that focuses on community-generated content.

These Web 2.0 sites have created a great opportunity to distribute your content in a blogging format. This will help generate links across highly visible websites with strong credibility in the eyes of Google.

Here is a list of 15 websites that can provide you with additional opportunities to distribute your content:

Page Rank	Site	Website URL
8	Squidoo	www.squidoo.com
8	Weebly	www.weebly.com
8	Live Journal	www.livejournal.com
8	Brave Net	www.bravenet.com
7	Blog Some	www.blogsome.com
7	Xanga	www.xanga.com
7	Tumblr	www.tumblr.com
6	Blog	www.blog.com
6	Hub Pages	www.hubpages.com
5	Blurty	www.blurty.com
5	Thoughts	www.thoughts.com
4	Blog Easy	www.blogeasy.com
4	Blog Studio	www.blogstudio.com
4	My New Blog	www.mynewblog.com
4	Free Blog It	www.freeblogit.com

As noted earlier in this book, Google gives websites a PageRank between one and ten, with a higher rank indicating more value placed on a given website.

Another opportunity in the blogging world is the creation of quality inbound links with forum participation. By participating in relevant conversations on various forums, you can establish yourself as an expert in your niche, driving greater awareness and increased traffic to your website while increasing your incoming links at the same time.

I highly recommend you go to a site such as Boardreader (**www.boardreader.com**) and do a search for forums that discuss your targeted topic. Once you identify a few that seem relevant, you should sign up and occasionally participate in the conversation. When you submit a comment, you should always have a link to your site placed within your signature. After you've submitted a few comments, the forum moderator will typically feel comfortable enough with your level of contribution to begin allowing the links to be picked up by Google, which will benefit your SEO efforts.

You can really make an impact on the search engines with a strong blogging and forum-participation strategy that helps you build a robust incoming linking profile.

- **SEO Challenge #8: Blog Set-Up**
  Set up a blog with either Blogger or WordPress. Did you choose to use their domain or set up your own?

- **Tools And Tricks**

  Blogging Content Management Systems (CMS)
  A blogging content management system is a free, web-based software program anyone can use to build and maintain a blog. It was originally intended as an easy way to set up a blog.

  - **WordPress (www.wordpress.com)**
  - **Blogger (www.blogger.com)**

  Blog Content Writing Services

These services can provide quality article writing and web content for a very low price. If you're in need of content to help market your website and are short on time, these services can be a great option.

- **iWriter (www.iwriter.com)**
- **99 Cent Articles (www.99centarticles.com)**
- **Article Ninjas (www.articleninjas.com)**
- **Articles on Tap (www.articlesontap.com)**
- **CC Articles (www.ccarticles.com)**

Hiring A Blog Content Writer

Businesses can use these websites to post jobs, search for freelance professionals, and solicit proposals. You can evaluate the contractors applying for the job by reviewing qualifications, work history, ratings, portfolios, and skill test scores.

- **Elance (www.elance.com)**
- **oDesk (www.odesk.com)**

Blogging Community Resources

- **Triberr (www.triberr.com)**

Triberr is an online blogging community using social media like Facebook, Twitter, Google Plus, and many others. Bloggers join similar groups or tribes and share each other's blogs and content. Bloggers on Triberr can provide comments on your blog as well.

- **Blogger Linkup (www.bloggerlinkup.com)**

When you join the Blogger Linkup list, you will receive weekly e-mails listing bloggers looking for expert sources and contributors for their already established blogs. When you see a request you want to fulfill, just respond directly to the requester. It's that easy.

- **My Blog Guest (www.myblogguest.com)**

My Blog Guest is a free community that connects guest bloggers to blog owners. By joining this community for free, you can gain tremendous exposure from guest posting opportunities.

- **Board Reader (www.boardreader.com)**

Board Reader is a search engine for forums and community boards. Simply type in a topic related to your website, and you will find all kinds of discussions you can contribute to, becoming an authority in your space and generating a stronger link profile. This can be a powerful method for obtaining links and gaining authority on the search engines.

Online Traffic Analysis

- **Alexa (www.alexa.com)**

Alexa computes traffic rankings by analyzing the web usage of millions of Alexa Toolbar users and data obtained from other diverse traffic data sources. The information is sorted, sifted, anonymized, counted, and computed to determine the traffic rankings shown in the Alexa service. This is a reliable and powerful information source for evaluating the traffic volumes of websites (especially if you're going to the trouble of contributing a blog post to a particular website).

Chapter 11

Report Card: A for Effort

So you've identified your key search terms, optimized your HTML tags, and diligently built out incoming links. You're regularly writing relevant articles with embedded anchor tags pointing back to your website, have bookmarked your site on all the biggest social sites, and are a regular contributor to your favorite forums and blogs.

Now how do you determine that all this hard work is paying off, that you're increasing in rankings and getting the return on investment you deserve for all of your efforts?

First, you'll want to check your rankings for the search terms you're targeting. Moz has a useful tool for this that is called Rank Tracker, and, as the name suggests, it tracks your keyword rankings.

When you launch your SEO endeavors, make sure you input the terms you're optimizing for into Rank Tracker or a similar tool. Then, you can see what kind of progress you've made and where you presently rank. This will help you when identifying priorities and evaluating progress across your campaign:

Search Term	URL	Engine/ Country	Latest Rank	Rank Change
marketing firms in Seattle	http://www.weareshowpony.com	Google / United States	8	↑18
Seattle branding agency	http://www.weareshowpony.com	Google / United States	15	↑23
Seattle creative agency	http://www.weareshowpony.com	Google / United States	12	↑8
Seattle ad agencies	http://www.weareshowpony.com	Google / United States	14	↑39

Since increasing search engine rankings is such a vital part of any SEO campaign, most of the major tool providers will allow you to check your rankings. If you want to use a free rank tracker tool, you can check out SEO Book (http://tools.seobook.com/firefox/rank-checker).

Some additional tool providers with rank-tracking abilities include:

- Authority Labs **(http://authoritylabs.com)**
- Raven Tools **(www.raventools.com)**
- WEbCEO **(www.webceo.com)**
- Market Samurai **(www.marketsamurai.com**)

Another great tool that can be utilized for free is Majestic SEO (**www.majesticseo.com**). It's important to note that there are paid and free versions of Majestic SEO. This tool works well for evaluating how your link-building efforts are working, and as we know, building links pointing back to your website will hugely influence how you rank in the search engines.

With Majestic SEO, you'll have the ability to review how your efforts are directly impacting your incoming links:

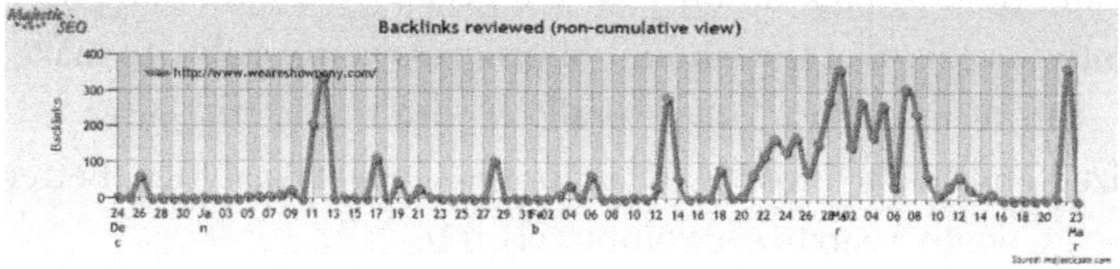

If you spend some time publishing a few articles to your favorite blogs and article sites, social bookmarking on a few targeted sites, submitting your site to niche directories, and building map citations to your website, the fluctuations in your incoming links will illustrate how these efforts are working. A spike in incoming links after a day focused on these efforts can indicate that the work you're putting in is truly starting to yield results.

Here is a look at how Majestic SEO will display data when pulling incoming links from a cumulative period of time:

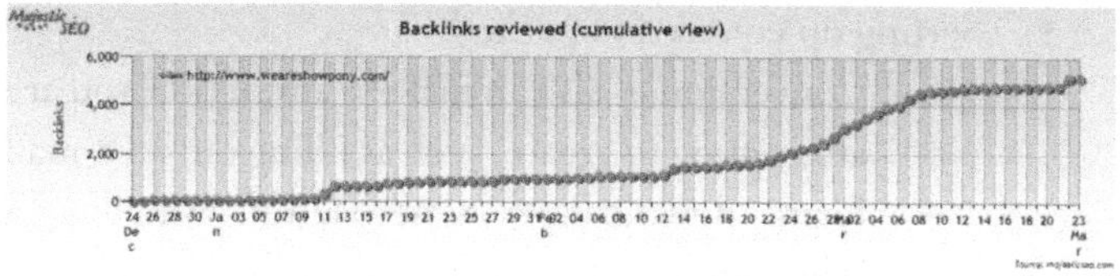

This level of information can be tremendously valuable in determining if the search engines are actually recognizing your link-acquiring efforts. Link building has a major impact on your overall online authority and ranking ability, so pay close attention to these reports to ensure the search engines are actually giving you credit for the links you're acquiring. It's important to note that it can take several months for your links to start accurately tracking in these tools. If you are not seeing immediate results, there is no need to despair. Give these tools some time to pick up on your efforts and you could be pleasantly surprised at the amount of progress you are able to make.

In terms of tracking overall website traffic, the most utilized and by far most popular tool is Google Analytics. Better yet, Google Analytics is completely free.

There is plenty of information available regarding how to properly set up Google Analytics for your website, so I won't give detailed instructions here (if only to save paper). Here is a good resource for detailed instructions:

http://www.google.com/analytics/learn/setup-checklist.html

Some of the things you'll want to focus on include:

- Installing tracking code
  - Creating and placing a conversion script throughout your website.

- Setting up conversion goals
  - Conversion goals can include any action you are attempting to create, such as filling out an e-mail form, downloading a newsletter, watching a sales video, or buying a product from your site.

When you first log into Google Analytics, you will see a visitor overview that includes the following information:

- Number of visitors

- Number of page views
- Average pages/visit
- Average visit duration
- Bounce rate (% of visitors that only see one page before exiting the website)
- Percentage of new visitors

All of this information serves to inform you of how many new visitors you're attracting and how engaged they are with your site when they land on it.

Once the conversion script is created and the goals are in place, you will have the ability to review reports that include all kinds of information about your website.

You can even set up a dashboard to include the specific areas you want to monitor. Some of the more prominent areas that advertisers tend to track include:

- Traffic sources (such as search traffic, direct traffic, and referral traffic).
- Conversion goals (such as goal completions, goal value, and goal conversion rate).

While I could show you how to access some of these reports, Google has provided so much information that it doesn't make sense to include a long instruction manual here. For more information, just visit the Google Analytics tutorial here:

http://www.google.com/analytics/learn/index.html

I'm a big advocate of Google Analytics, as it is free and provides very detailed information about your online metrics. In addition to Google Analytics, it's important to diligently track how your search terms are ranking and what kinds of requests are coming through your site so you can get the best information possible about what is actually driving your increased traffic and sales.

I take reporting very seriously. After all, it's difficult to pinpoint what is working well and what needs adjustment if you're not meticulously tracking your progress and gaining insight into how these efforts are translating into real-world results, such as more customers, sales, visitors, and increased online visibility.

There are tons of great tools available to provide more insight into what is taking place on your site and how visitors are finding you. The tools described in this chapter can be great resources, but there are many others as well. I recommend that any website owner initially set up Google Analytics, as it is free and provides some crucial information about your website's traffic. You should also leverage the free version of Majestic SEO if you don't want to spend money on the paid version. It's very possible that these free tools will be sufficient for your reporting needs.

So, by all means, start with the free tools, and if your traffic grows, if you start experimenting with different types of marketing, or if you need more details about how you're being found online, you can evaluate and test some of the other resources out there. Here are some additional powerful and popular analytics tools you can evaluate for tracking purposes:

- SpyFu Recon (**www.spyfu.com/recon**)
- Optify (**www.optify.net**)
- Clicky (**www.getclicky.com**)
- Piwik (**www.piwik.org**)
- Omniture (**www.omniture.com**)
- WebTrends (**www.webtrends.com**)

I spend a decent amount of time and resources on reporting for my SEO efforts and you should too. This type of information can be incredibly valuable when attempting to quantify your efforts and realizing actual value created from these SEO activities. After all, in business, time is money. If your SEO efforts are done properly, they can translate into a substantial return on your investment of time and resources.

➢ **SEO Challenge #9: Analytics Set-Up**
Set up Google Analytics across your website and make sure you track every single page. Refer back to the set-up guides in this chapter for guidance. Was it more or less difficult than you expected?

➢ **Tools And Tricks**

Rank Tracking Tools
Rank tracking tools are designed to retrieve search engine rankings for pages and keywords. Most will also allow you to track selected rankings over time. Rank tracking can be a useful way to help validate progress toward your SEO goals. After all, it's impossible to know if your SEO efforts are working if you're not able to track your progress. Here are some great rank tracking tools for this purpose:

- **Moz (www.moz.com)**
- **SEO Book (http://tools.seobook.com)**
- **Authority Labs (http://authoritylabs.com)**
- **Raven Tools (www.raventools.com)**
- **WebCEO (www.webceo.com)**
- **Market Samurai (www.marketsamurai.com)**

Link Tracking Tools
Majestic SEO (www.majesticseo.com)

Find out how all the websites on the Internet link to each other with the largest link intelligence database on the planet. This site gives you an insane amount of detailed information about links, which can be invaluable for fully understanding how your link-building efforts are working.

Analytics Tools
Website analytics not only measure web traffic but can also be used for business and market research and to assess and improve the effectiveness of a website. Installing analytics will help you estimate how traffic to your website changes based on the work you put into building awareness and increasing visitors. Analytics can provide information about many areas of your website, including overall website traffic, the channels driving new visitors, the length of time your audience is staying on your website, and specific actions your potential customers are taking when they get to your website. Here are some great tools to help you track your analytics:

- **Google Analytics (www.google.com/analytics)**
- **SpyFu Recon (www.spyfu.com/recon)**
- **Optify (www.optify.net)**
- **Clicky (www.getclicky.com)**
- **Piwik (www.piwik.org)**
- **Omniture (www.omniture.com)**
- **WebTrends (www.webtrends.com)**

Chapter 12

The Step-by-Step SEO Method

Now that we've covered in detail how to effectively set up and manage a search engine optimization campaign, it's time to put together a plan of action utilizing all of the new tools and resources in our arsenal. The goal with this plan is to put enough arrows in your quiver to effectively hit your target. If followed diligently, it should help lead you to the results you desire.

I will warn you that the number one reason people fail at SEO is because they give up too quickly. If you don't see results in the first month or two, don't give up! It could happen very suddenly, where you go from relative obscurity to Google's first page, even if it feels as though nothing is happening. Stick with the plan and give it the appropriate amount of time to work its magic. Patience will be your biggest ally in your quest to achieve stellar search engine rankings and increased website traffic.

Now that you've had your pep talk, here is how the plan of action should look going forward:

Step 1 – Keyword Selection

Select keywords to target in your SEO campaign. This should initially include five to ten search terms. These terms should have a difficulty score in the lower to middle range with any of the recommended keyword tools. The terms should also enjoy a healthy amount of monthly search volume according to the Google Keyword Tool. Ideally, you would like keywords that receive at least one thousand searches per month. Depending on your specific area of focus, though, this may be an unrealistic goal. Select your target terms and then enter them in an Excel spreadsheet in order of priority. Keep this Excel file on hand for future reference.

Step 2 – Onsite Optimization

Using your selected keywords, revise the following tags on your website to include your target search terms:

- Update header tag <H1>
- Update title tag <Title>
- Update meta description
- Update on-page content
    - Include target search terms in top twenty-five words and bottom twenty-five words on page and bold them once.

- Remove meta keyword tag
- Include subpages
    - For any important keywords that you want to rank with, create a subpage with relevant information and a domain that includes the keyword. For example, if you want to target "Seattle roofing," write some content related to that with a domain like: **www.roofer.com/seattleroofing.html**

- Check for onsite errors or issues
    - Once your site has incorporated the proper changes, use any of the recommended tools as well as your Google Webmaster Tools to identify how optimized your page is for your target keywords. If you receive errors or recommendations, make the implied changes and test again until you are satisfied with your website.

Step 3 – Link-Building Activities

- Create map citations
    - Go through the provided list and fill out local map directories for your business if you are going after any location-specific searches (at least ten directories per month).

- Create and distribute articles
    - o Set up at least five to ten accounts with some of the article directories provided in this book. Then write or post at least five articles per month that include your target search terms with anchor links pointing back to your website.

- Create and distribute press releases
    - o Create one press release on a newsworthy topic, such as a new service you're offering or promotion you're running, by writing a short blurb about the exciting changes taking place. Then submit to PRLog or PRWeb with the appropriate links embedded in the press release. I recommend sending out one press release every month.

- Practice competitive link building
    - o Conduct a Google search for your top targeted keyword. Next, take note of the websites currently enjoying the top positioning for this term. Then leverage any of the tools that you decide to use and enter the first website you discovered. This will then return a list of current sites linking back to the website in question. Finally, identify at least ten websites that would be a good fit as a link partner and reach out via e-mail, asking them to link to your site.

- Use social bookmarking
  - Go through the list of social bookmarking sites provided in this book and fill out at least ten different social bookmarking accounts per month.

- Social media posting
  - Write a few relevant posts about your business or industry on your Facebook page and make a conscious effort to increase fans and likes on your page. Also, ensure that you're actively using Tweet Adder or implementing another method to increase your Twitter reach while building a strong network. Don't forget to focus some attention on Google Plus as well, working to increase the number of people "circling" you to boost your social status in the eyes of Google.

- Submit to directories
  - Go through the list of directories provided in this book and fill out at least ten different directory profiles from sites on the list with the highest page rankings.

- Blogging and forum commenting
  - After you've set up your very own blog through WordPress or Blogger, write one article per week related to your business and target keywords. Make sure you use Blogger Link Up

to contribute a blog post every month to an outside blog so that you can differentiate your blogging strategy. Make sure to increase your blog exposure by extending your reach through Triberr. Also, make sure that you log into BoardReader at least once a month to submit comments on relevant forums.

- Set up reporting
    - Set up a free Google Analytics account and make sure you are tracking activity across your website.
    - Track your keyword rankings with any of the tools mentioned in this book to evaluate your ranking increases stemming from these activities.
    - Log into Google Analytics and/or Majestic SEO every couple of weeks to verify any progress with link acquisition and online traffic increases.

Follow this step-by-step guide and you will be effectively optimizing your website for the major search engines. Keep a tracking sheet on hand and mark your progress every month. It should look something like this:

✓ Keyword Development
✓ Onsite Optimization
✓ Ten Local Map Citations
✓ Five Articles Written and Distributed
✓ One Press Release Written and Distributed

- ✓ Ten Competitor Link Partners Contacted
- ✓ Ten Social Bookmarking Submissions
- ✓ Four Facebook Posts
- ✓ Two Tweets
- ✓ Two Google Plus Posts
- ✓ Ten Directory Submissions
- ✓ Four Blog Posts Written and Distributed
- ✓ Ten Forum Comments Submitted

Based on my experience, following a schedule like this will typically require around five hours per week on an ongoing basis. However, you can successfully manage these SEO activities with less of a time commitment by utilizing some of the resources outlined in this book to help with the content writing for your website. While this may seem like a big commitment, getting onto Google's first page for just a handful of terms will typically more than justify the time and/or expense required to implement this plan.

Here is a calendar you can follow to better track your link-building efforts on your campaigns:

Monthly SEO Schedule

Sunday	Monday	Tuesday	Wednesday	Thursday	Friday	Saturday
1	2 5 Social Bookmarking Submissions	3 Blog Post Twitter Post FB Post	4 5 Competitor Linking Sites Contacted	5 Article Submission	6 5 Local Map Citations	7
8	9 Article Submission	10 5 Directory Submissions	11 10 Forum Comments Posted	12 Blog Post Google+ Post FB Post	13 Article Submission	14
15	16 Review Reporting	17 Blog Post Twitter Post FB Post	18 5 Directory Submissions	19 5 Local Map Citations	20 Article Submission	21
22	23 5 Competitor Linking Sites Contacted	24 Article Submission	25 5 Social Bookmarking Submissions	26 Blog Post Google+ Post FB Post	27 Press Release	28
29	30 Review Reporting					

When it comes to SEO—or any worthwhile activity, for that matter—the more effort you put in, the more you will get out of it. Therefore, if you can find the time and resources to go above and beyond the recommended SEO plan, it will benefit your search engine traffic in the long run.

Conversely, even doing a little of this work is better than doing nothing at all when it comes to helping your online presence. Just keep in mind that while engaging in these activities on a reduced schedule will still work, it is likely to increase the amount of time it will take for you to start seeing results. If you don't have the time or desire to write content yourself, then I highly recommend you hire an outside company or contractor to assist with these activities.

There you have it. The Step-by-Step plan that can help you soar from obscurity to authority on the search engines.

- **SEO Challenge #10: Implement an SEO Program**

  Give the Step-by-Step method a serious try for three months. Follow the program closely and consistently. When possible, go above and beyond the recommended work outlined in this plan. How much movement did you experience on the search engines after three months? How many additional visitors have you attracted to your site with this process?

Conclusion

Go Forth and Take the Search Engines by Storm

Nothing ventured, nothing gained, so the saying goes. Give this process a try, as you have nothing to lose. While it's impossible to guarantee success (or everyone would be successful), I can assure you that this process has led to some huge successes for the campaigns I've personally worked on. Work at it just a few hours a week and over the course of a few months, you could be pleasantly surprised with the results you experience on the search engines.

What can you expect? Here is a breakdown of how my past campaigns have typically progressed. First, there is a slight increase in rankings for some of the search terms being targeted. Typically, like clockwork, after about two or three months, a few key search terms will start to rank and, as progress is made, these search terms will eventually make it onto the first page of the major search engines.

From my experience, by the time some of the targeted search terms reach the top half of Google's first page, there has been a big increase in online traffic. As mentioned earlier in this book, you can find some free tools to track this traffic through Google Analytics (**http://www.google.com/analytics**). Better yet, because this traffic has been so targeted and relevant, these increases have led to more sales, phone calls, and other conversions.

Additionally, there was a strong correlation between the search terms being optimized and the keywords driving the majority of the traffic online. This strong connection was not a coincidence.

If you're still not sure SEO is worth the effort, here are some key reasons why you should give search engine optimization some serious consideration:

- SEO is important because it improves the odds of someone finding you online.
- Online visibility can bolster your credibility and brand awareness.
- SEO can put you in front of people actively looking for your products and services.
- SEO allows you to focus your online marketing efforts on an end result, such as more sales, leads, and visibility.

What makes search engine optimization such a powerful method of advertising is that it empowers your customers to find you at the exact moment they are actively looking for what you have to offer. Most other advertising channels require you to shout your messaging at prospective customers and simply hope for the best.

Better yet, while most advertising requires you to invest money based on the number of people you are attempting to get in front of, the customers you attract with SEO are completely free when you begin to get placement on the search engines:

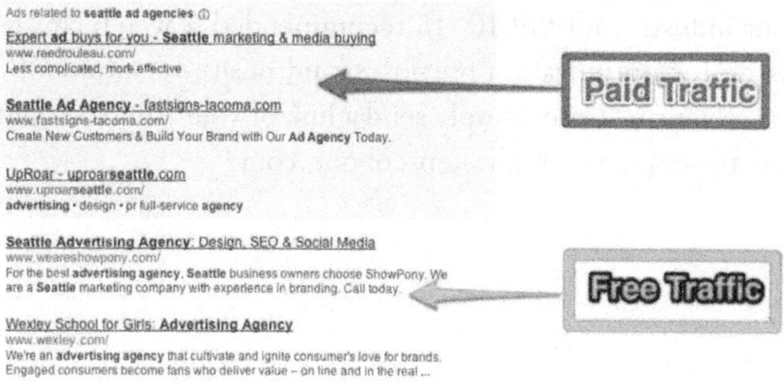

Which would you prefer? If your answer is free customers, I think you're starting to see the value in this!

I urge you to give this strategy a try. With the Step-by-Step process—which includes all the tools and resources needed—it is easy to put theory into practice.

Free marketing and website traffic is there for the taking—as long as you know how to get it. And now *you* know how to get it! So go forth and conquer the search engines. Once you move forward, you'll never look back. The days of the yellow pages are behind us. It's a new kind of revolution—and information is king.

A Humble Request

I would like to thank you for reading *Step-by-Step SEO*. If you feel this book has provided value, please visit Amazon.com and write a review.

I'm always looking for feedback and would love for you to be part of the SEO community. I will provide anyone who completes a review with a website evaluation—absolutely *free*! This evaluation includes an overview of the competitive landscape in your industry, a list of 10–15 recommended search terms to focus on for optimization purposes, and onsite recommendations for your website. Simply send a link of your Amazon.com review to support@stepbystepseobook.com.

Glossary of Essential SEO Terms

#

301 Moved Permanently

The file has been moved permanently to a new location. This is the preferred method of redirecting for most pages or websites. If you are going to move an entire site to a new location, you may want to test moving a file or folder first. If that ranks well, then proceed with moving the entire site. Depending on your site authority and crawl frequency, it may take anywhere from a few days to a month or so for the 301 redirect to be picked up.

404 Not Found

The server was unable to locate the URL. However, some content management systems send 404 status codes when documents do exist.

A

Above the Fold

A term traditionally used to describe the top portion of a newspaper. In e-mail or web marketing, it means the area of content viewable prior to scrolling.

AdWords

Google's advertisement and link auction network, which controls all search engine listings found in the sponsored section of Google.

Affiliate Marketing

Affiliate marketing programs allow merchants to expand their market reach and mindshare by paying independent agents on a cost per action (CPA) basis. Affiliates only get paid if visitors complete an action.

Age

Some social networks or search systems may take site age, page age, user account age, and related historical data into account when determining how much to trust that person, website, or document. Some specialty search engines, like blog search engines, may also boost the relevancy of new documents.

Alexa

Amazon.com-owned search service which measures website traffic. While not highly accurate, it is free.

Alt Attribute

Most major search engines are not able to easily distinguish an image's content. Using an image alt attribute allows you to help search engines understand the function of an image by providing a text equivalent for the object.

Analytics

Software that allows you to track your page views, user paths, and conversion statistics based upon interpretation of your log files or through including a JavaScript tracking code on your site.

Anchor Text

The text a user would click on to follow a link.

Search engines assume that your page is authoritative for the words that people include in links pointing at your site. When links occur naturally, they typically have a wide array of anchor text combinations. Too much similar anchor text may be considered a sign of manipulation and could thus be discounted or filtered. Make sure to mix up your anchor text when building links that you control.

API (Application Program Interface)

A series of conventions or routines used to access software functions. Most major search products have an API program.

Ask

Ask is a search engine owned by InterActive Corp. It was originally named Ask Jeeves; "Jeeves" was dumped in early 2006.

Authority

The ability of a page or domain to rank well in search engines. Five key factors associated with site and page authority are link equity, site age, traffic trends, site history, and the publishing of unique, original, quality content. Search engines constantly tweak their algorithms to try to balance relevancy algorithms based on topical authority and overall authority across the entire web.

B

Backlink (see Inbound Link)

Bait and Switch

Marketing technique where you make something look overtly pure or as though it has another purpose to get people to believe in it or vote for it (by linking to it or sharing it with friends), then switch the intent or purpose of the website after you gain authority. For example, it is generally easier to get links to informational websites than commercial sites. Some new sites might gain authority much more quickly if they tried looking noncommercial and gained influence before trying to monetize their market position.

Black Hat SEO

Search engines set up guidelines that help them extract billions of dollars of ad revenue from the work of publishers and the attention of searchers. Within that highly profitable framework, search engines consider certain marketing techniques deceptive in nature and label them as black hat SEO. Those considered within the guidelines are called white hat SEO techniques. The search guidelines are not a static set of rules, and things that may be considered legitimate one day may be considered deceptive the next.

Blog

A periodically updated journal, typically formatted in reverse chronological order. Many blogs not only archive and categorize information, but also provide a feed and allow simple user interaction like leaving comments on the posts. Most blogs tend to be personal in nature. Blogs are generally quite authoritative, with heavy link equity, because they give people a reason to frequently come back to the site, read the content, and link to whatever they think is interesting.

Blogger

Blogger is a free blog platform owned by Google.

It allows you to publish sites on a subdomain of Blogspot.com or to your own domain. **If you are serious about building a brand or making money online, you should publish your content to your own domain** because it can be hard to reclaim a website's link equity and age-related trust if you have built years of link equity into a subdomain on someone else's website.

Bold

A way to make words appear in a bolder font. Words that appear in a bolder font are more likely to be read by humans scanning a page. A search engine may also place slightly greater weight on these words than regular text. When writing your own copy, if a word or phrase appears on a page many times, it does not make sense or look natural to bold every occurrence.

Bookmarks

Most browsers come with the ability to bookmark your favorite pages. Many web-based services also allow you to bookmark and share your favorite resources. The popularity of a document (as measured in terms of link equity, number of bookmarks, or usage data) is a signal for the quality of the information. Some search engines may be using bookmarks to aid their search relevancy.

Brand

The emotional response associated with your company and/or products. A brand is built through controlling customer expectations and the social interactions between customers. Building a brand is what allows you to move away from commodity-based pricing and toward higher margin, value-based pricing.

Branded Keywords

Keywords or keyword phrases associated with a brand. Typically, branded searches occur late in the buying cycle and are some of the highest-value and highest-converting keywords.

Broken Link

A hyperlink that is not functioning. A link that does not lead to the desired location.

Browser

Client used to view the World Wide Web. The most popular browsers are Microsoft's Internet Explorer, Mozilla's Firefox, Safari, and Opera.

C

Cache

Copy of a web page stored by a search engine. When you search the web, you are not actively searching the whole web, but files in the search engine index.

Canonical URL

Many content management systems are configured with errors that cause duplicate or exceptionally similar content to get indexed under multiple URLs. Many webmasters use inconsistent link structures throughout their site that cause the exact same content to get indexed under multiple URLs. The canonical version of any URL is the single most authoritative version indexed by major search engines. Search engines typically use PageRank or a similar measure to determine which version of a URL is the canonical URL.

Cloaking

Displaying different content to search engines than to searchers. Depending on the intent of the display discrepancy and the strength of the brand of the person or company cloaking, it may be considered reasonable or it may get a site banned from a search engine.

Clustering

In search results, the listings from any individual site are typically limited to a certain number and grouped together to make the search results appear neat and organized and to ensure diversity amongst the top-ranked results.

Comments

Many blogs and other content management systems allow readers to leave user feedback. Leaving enlightening and thoughtful comments on someone else's related website is one way to get them to notice you.

Conceptual Links

Links that search engines attempt to understand beyond just their words. Some rather advanced search engines attempt to find out the concept links versus just matching the words of the text to that specific word set.

Concept Search

A search that attempts to conceptually match results with the query, not necessarily with those words, but rather their concept.

Conversion

Many forms of online advertising are easy to track. A conversion is reached when a desired goal is completed.

Most offline ads have generally been much harder to track than online ads. Some marketers use custom phone numbers or coupon codes to tie offline activity to online marketing.

Here are a few common example desired goals:

- a product sale
- completion of a lead form
- a phone call
- capture of an e-mail
- completion of a survey
- capture of a person's attention
- feedback
- website share by a visitor
- link at your site by a site visitor

Copyright

The legal right to publish and reproduce a particular piece of work.

Cookie

Small data file written to a user's local machine to track them. Cookies are used to help websites customize your user experience and track conversions.

CPA (Cost Per Action)

The effectiveness of many forms of online advertising is measured on a cost-per-action basis.

CPC (Cost Per Click)

Many search ads and contextually targeted ads are sold in auctions where the advertiser is charged a certain cost per click.

CPM

Cost per thousand impressions. Many people use CPM as a measure of how profitable a website is or has the potential of becoming.

Crawl Depth

How deeply a website is crawled and indexed. Since searches that are longer in nature tend to be more targeted, it is important to try to get most or all of a site indexed such that the deeper pages have the ability to rank for relevant long-tail keywords.

Crawl Frequency

How frequently a website is crawled. Sites that are well trusted or frequently updated may be crawled more often than sites with low trust scores and limited link authority.

Click Through Rate (CTR)

The percentage of people who view and then click on an advertisement, which is a way to measure how relevant a traffic source or keyword is.

D

Dead Link

A link that is no longer functional. Most large, high-quality websites have at least a few dead links in them, but the ratio of good links to dead links can be seen as a sign of information quality.

Deep Link

A link that points to an internal page within a website. When links grow naturally, most high-quality websites have many links pointing at interior pages. When you request links from other websites, it makes sense to request a link from their most targeted relevant page to your most targeted relevant page. Some webmasters even create content based on easy linking opportunities.

Dedicated Server

Server limited to serving one website or a small collection of websites owned by a single person. Dedicated servers tend to be more reliable than shared (or virtual) servers. Dedicated servers usually run from $100 to $500 a month. Virtual servers typically run from $5 to $50 per month.

De-Listing

Temporarily or permanently becoming de-indexed from a directory or search engine.

Demographics

Statistical data or characteristics that define segments of a population.

Description

Directories and search engines provide a short description near each listing that aims to add context to the title.

High-quality directories typically prefer the description describe what the site is about rather than something overtly promotional.

Directory

A categorized catalog of websites, typically manually organized by topical editorial experts. Some directories cater to specific niche topics, while others are more comprehensive in nature. Major search engines likely place significant weight on links from DMOZ and the Yahoo! Directory. Smaller and less established general directories likely pull less weight. If a directory does not exercise editorial control over listings, search engines will not be likely to trust its links at all.

Domain

Scheme used for logical or location organization of the web. Many people also use the word domain to refer to a specific website.

Duplicate Content

Content duplicate or near duplicate in nature.

Search engines do not want to index multiple versions of similar content. Many automated content-generation techniques rely on recycling content, so some search engines are somewhat strict in filtering out content they deem to be similar or nearly duplicate.

E

Editorial Link

Search engines count links as votes of quality. They primarily want to count editorial links that were earned over links that were bought or bartered. If the links are from sites without editorial control, like link farms, they are not likely to help you rank well.

Entry Page

The page a visitor uses to enter your site. If you are link building, it is important to point links at your most appropriate page when possible.

Ethical SEO

Search engines like to paint SEO services that manipulate their relevancy algorithms as being unethical. Any particular technique is generally not associated with ethics, but is either effective or ineffective.

Everflux

Major search indexes are constantly updating. Google refers to this continuous refresh as everflux. In the past, Google updated their index roughly once a month. Those updates were named Google Dances, but since Google shifted to a constantly updating index, Google no longer does what was traditionally called a Google Dance.

External Link

A link that references another domain. If you link out to lots of low-quality sites or primarily rely on low-quality reciprocal links, some search engines may not rank your site very well. Search engines are more likely to trust high-quality editorial links (both to and from your site).

F

Favorites (see Bookmarks)

Feed

Many content management systems, such as blogs, allow readers to subscribe to content update notifications via RSS or XML feeds. Feeds can also refer to pay per click, syndicated feeds, or merchant product feeds. Merchant product feeds have become less effective as a means of content generation due to improving duplicate content filters.

Flash

Vector graphics-based animation software that makes it easier for websites to look rich and interactive. Search engines tend to struggle with indexing and ranking Flash websites because Flash typically contains so little relevant content.

Forward Links (see Outbound Links)

Fresh Content

Content that is dynamic in nature and gives people a reason to keep paying attention to your website. Fresh content often refers to creating new content.

FTP (File Transfer Protocol)

A protocol for transferring data between computers. Many content management systems (such as blogging platforms) include FTP capabilities.

G

Google Advertising Professional (GAP)

A program that qualifies marketers as proficient AdWords marketers.

Google

The world's leading search engine in terms of reach. Google pioneered search by analyzing linkage data via PageRank. Google was created by Stanford students Larry Page and Sergey Brin.

Google Bot

Google's search engine spider. Google has a shared crawl cache between their various spiders, including vertical search spiders and spiders associated with ad targeting.

Google Bombing

Making a page rank well for a specific search query by pointing hundreds or thousands of links at it with the keywords in the anchor text.

Google Bowling

Knocking a competitor out of the search results by pointing hundreds or thousands of low-trust, low-quality links at their website. Typically, it is easier to bowl new sites out of the results. Older, established sites are much harder to knock out of the search results.

Google Dance

In the past, Google updated their index roughly once a month. Those updates were named Google Dances, but since Google shifted to a constantly updating index, Google no longer does what was traditionally called a Google Dance.

Major search indexes are constantly updating. Google refers to this continuous refresh as everflux.

Google Keyword Tool

Keyword research tool provided by Google that estimates the traffic and competition for a keyword and will tell you what keywords Google thinks are relevant to your site or a page on your site.

Google Sitemaps

Program that webmasters can use to help Google index their sites' content. Please note that the best way to submit your site to search engines and keep it in their search indexes is to build high-quality editorial links.

Guestbook Spam

A type of low-quality automated link in which search engines do not place much trust.

H

Headings

The heading element briefly describes the subject of the section it introduces. Heading elements are classified from H1 to H6, with the lower-numbered headings being most important. You should only use a single H1 element on each page, though you may want to use multiples of the other heading elements to structure a document.

Headline

The title of an article or story.

Hidden Text

SEO technique used to show search engine spiders text that human visitors do not see. While some sites may get away with it for a while, generally the risk-to-reward ratio is inadequate for most legitimate sites to consider using hidden text.

HITS

Link-based algorithm that ranks relevancy scores based on citations from topical authorities.

Home Page

The main page on your website, which is largely responsible for helping develop your brand and setting up the navigational schemes used to help visitors and search engines navigate your website. As far as SEO goes, a home page is typically going to be one of the easier pages to rank for some of your more competitive terms, largely because it is easy to build links into a home page. You should ensure your home page stays focused and reinforces your brand, though, and do not assume that most of your visitors will come to your site via the home page. If your site is well structured, many pages will likely be far more popular and rank better than your home page for relevant queries.

Host (see Server)

HTML (Hypertext Markup Language)

The language in which pages on the World Wide Web are created.

HTTP (Hypertext Transfer Protocol)

The foremost protocol to communicate between servers and web browsers. Hypertext transfer protocol is the means by which data is transferred from its residing location on a server to an active browser.

I

Inbound Link

Link pointing to one website from another website.

Most search engines allow you to see a sample of links pointing to a document by searching using the link function.

Index

A collection of data used as a searchable bank to find a match to a user-fed query. The larger search engines have billions of documents in their catalogs.

Internal Link

Link from one page on a site to another page on the same site. It is preferable to use descriptive internal linking to make it easy for search engines to understand what your website is about. Use consistent navigational anchor text for each section of your site, emphasizing other pages within that section. Place links to relevant related pages within the content area of your site to help further show the relationship between pages and improve the usability of your website.

Internet

Vast worldwide network of connected computers.

Internet Explorer

Microsoft's web browser.

IP Address (Internet Protocol Address)

Every computer connected to the Internet has an IP address. Some websites and servers have unique IP addresses, but most web hosts host multiple websites on a single host.

ISP (Internet Service Provider)

ISPs sell end users access to the web. Some of these companies also sell usage data to web analytics companies.

<u>J</u>

JavaScript

A client-side scripting language that can be embedded into HTML documents to add dynamic features.

<u>K</u>

Keyword

A word or phrase implying a certain mindset or demand that targeted prospects are likely to search for. Long-tail and brand-related keywords are generally worth more than shorter and vague keywords because they typically occur later in the buying cycle and are associated with a greater level of implied intent.

Keyword Density

An old measure of search engine relevancy based on how prominent keywords appeared within the content of a page. Keyword density is no longer a valid measure of relevancy over a broad open search index, though. When people use keyword-stuffed copy, it tends to read mechanically (and thus does not convert well and is not link-worthy), plus some pages crafted with just the core keyword in mind often lack semantically related words and modifiers from the related vocabulary (and that causes the pages to rank poorly as well).

Keyword Funnel

The relationship between searchers' various related keywords. Some searches are particularly well aligned with others due to spelling errors, poor search relevancy, and automated or manual query refinement.

Keyword Research

The process of discovering relevant keywords and keyword phrases to focus your SEO marketing campaigns on.

Keyword Research Tools

Tools that help you discover potential keywords based on past search volumes, search trends, bid prices, and page content from related websites.

Keyword Stuffing

Writing copy that uses excessive amounts of the core keyword. When people use keyword-stuffed copy, it tends to read mechanically (and thus does not convert well and is not linkworthy), plus some pages crafted with just the core keyword in mind often lack semantically related words and modifiers from the related vocabulary (and that causes the pages to rank poorly as well).

L

Landing Page

The page on which a visitor arrives after clicking on a link or advertisement.

Link

A citation from one web document to another web document or another position in the same document. Most major search engines consider links a vote of trust.

Link Baiting

The art of targeting, creating, and formatting information to provoke the target audience to point high-quality links at your site. Many link-baiting techniques are targeted at social media and bloggers.

Link Building

The process of building high-quality linkage data that search engines will use to evaluate your website as authoritative, relevant, and trustworthy.

Link Bursts

A rapid increase in the quantity of links pointing at a website. When links occur naturally, they generally develop over time. In some cases, it may make sense that popular viral articles receive many links quickly, but there are typically other signs of quality as well.

Link Churn

The rate at which a site loses links.

Link Equity

A measure of a site's strength based on its inbound link popularity and the authority of the sites providing those links.

Link Farm

Website or group of websites that exercise little to no editorial control when linking to other sites.

Log Files

Server files that show your leading sources of traffic and what people are searching for to find your website.

Link Hoarding

A method of trying to keep all your link popularity by not linking out to other sites. Generally, link hoarding is a bad idea.

Link Popularity

The number of links pointing at a website. For competitive search queries, link quality counts much more than link quantity. Google typically shows a smaller sample of known linkage data than the other engines do, even though Google still counts many of the links they do not show when you do a link search.

Link Reputation

The combination of your link equity and anchor text.

Link Rot

A measure of how many and what percentage of a website's links are broken.

Long Tail

Long-tail keywords are longer strings of search terms that offer more precise and specific searches, thus have a higher value.

M

Manual Review

All major search engines combine a manual review process with their automated relevancy algorithms to help catch search spam and train their relevancy algorithms. Abnormal usage data or link growth patterns may also flag sites for manual review.

Meta Description

The meta description tag is typically a sentence or two describing the content of the page.

Meta Keywords

The meta keywords tag can be used to highlight keywords and keyword phrases that the page is targeting. Many people spammed meta keyword tags and searchers typically never see the tag, so most search engines do not place much (if any) weight on it. Many SEO professionals no longer use meta keywords tags.

Meta Search

A search engine that pulls top-ranked results from other search engines and rearranges them into a new result set.

Meta Tags

People generally refer to meta descriptions and meta keywords as meta tags. Some people also group the page title in with these.

Mindshare

A measure of the amount of people who think of you or your product when considering products in your category.

Sites with strong mindshare, top rankings, or a strong memorable brand are far more likely to be linked to than sites that are less memorable and have less search exposure. The link quality of mindshare-related links most likely exceeds the quality of the average link on the web. If you sell noncommodities, personal recommendations also typically carry far greater weight than search rankings alone.

Mirror Site

Site that mirrors (or duplicates) the contents of another website. Generally, search engines prefer not to index duplicate content.

N

Navigation

Scheme to help website users understand where they are, where they have been, and how that relates to the rest of your website.

Niche

A topic or subject that a website is focused on.

Search is a broad field, but as you drill down, each niche consists of many smaller niches.

Nofollow

Attribute used to prevent a link from passing link authority. Commonly used on sites with user-generated content, like in blog comments.

O

Organic Search Results

Most major search engines' results consist of paid ads and unpaid listings. The unpaid/algorithmic listings are called the organic search results. Organic search results are organized by relevancy, which is largely determined based on linkage data, page content, usage data, and historical domain and trust-related data. Most clicks on search results are on the organic search results. Some studies have shown that 70 to 80 percent or more of clicks are on the organic search results.

Outbound Link

A link from one website pointing at another external website.

P

PageRank

Algorithmic scale based on link equity that estimates the importance of web documents. Since PageRank is widely tied to Google's relevancy algorithms, other engines have moved away from relying on PageRank and place more emphasis on trusted links via algorithms such as TrustRank.

Page Title (see Title)

Paid Inclusion

A method of allowing websites that pass editorial quality guidelines to buy relevant exposure.

Paid Link (see Text Link Ads)

Penalty

Search engines prevent some websites suspected of spamming from ranking highly in the results by banning or penalizing them. These penalties may be automated algorithmically or manually applied. If a site is penalized algorithmically, it may start ranking again after a certain period once the reason for being penalized is fixed. If a site is penalized manually, the penalty may last an exceptionally long time or require contacting the search engine with a reinclusion request to remedy.

Personalization

Altering the search results based on a person's location, search history, content recently viewed, or other factors relevant to the individual on a personal level.

Portal

Website offering common consumer services such as news, e-mail, other content, and search.

PPC (Pay Per Click)

A pricing model through which most search ads and many contextual ad programs are sold. PPC ads only charge advertisers if a potential customer clicks on an ad.

Q

Quality Content

Content that is link-worthy in nature.

Quality Link

Search engines consider links votes of trust. Quality links count more than low-quality links.

Query

The actual "search string" a searcher enters into a search engine.

Query Refinement

Some searchers may refine their search query if they deem the results irrelevant. Query refinement is both a manual and an automated process. If searchers do not find their search results relevant, they may search again. Search engines may also automatically refine queries

R

Reciprocal Links

Nepotistic link exchanges where websites try to build false authority by trading links, using three-way link trades, or other low-quality link schemes.

Redirect

A method of alerting browsers and search engines that a page location moved. Permanent changes of location use 301 redirects, and 302 redirects are used for a temporary change of location.

Registrar

A company that allows you to register domain names.

Reinclusion

If a site has been penalized for spamming, the webmaster may fix the infraction and ask for reinclusion. Depending on the severity of the infraction and the brand strength of the site, they may or may not be added to the search index.

Referrer

The source from which a website visitor came.

Relevancy

A measure of how useful searchers find search results.

Many search engines may also bias organic search results to informational resources since commercial ads also appear in the search results.

Robots.txt

A file that sits in the root of a site and tells search engines which files not to crawl. Some search engines will still list your URLs as URL-only listings, even if you block them using a robots.txt file.

ROI (Return on Investment)

A measure of how much return you receive from each marketing dollar. While ROI is a fairly sophisticated measurement, some search marketers prefer to account for their marketing using even more sophisticated profit elasticity calculations.

RSS (Rich Site Summary or Real Simple Syndication)

A method of syndicating information to a feed reader or other software that allows people to subscribe to a channel they are interested in.

S

Search History

Many search engines store user search history information. This data can be used for better ad targeting or to make old information more findable. Search engines may also determine what a document is about and how much they trust a domain based on aggregate usage data.

Search Engine

A tool or device used to find relevant information. Search engines consist of a spider, index, relevancy algorithms, and search results.

SEM (Search Engine Marketing)

Marketing a website in search engines, typically via SEO, buying pay-per-click ads and paid inclusion.

SEO (Search Engine Optimization)

The art and science of publishing information and marketing it in a manner that helps search engines understand that your information is relevant to related search queries. SEO consists largely of keyword research, SEO copywriting, information architecture, link building, brand building, mindshare building, reputation management, and viral marketing.

SEO Copywriting

Writing and formatting copy in a way that will make it appear relevant to a wide array of related search queries.

SERP (Search Engine Results Page)

The page on which search engines show the results for a search query.

Search Marketing

Marketing a website in search engines, typically via SEO, buying pay-per-click ads and paid inclusion.

Sitemap

Page that can be used to help give search engines a secondary route to navigate through your site.

Social Media

Websites that allow users to create valuable content that can be shared virally. A few examples of social media sites are social bookmarking sites and social news sites.

Spam

Unsolicited e-mail messages. Search engines also like to outsource their relevancy issues by calling low-quality search results spam. They have vague, ever-changing guidelines that determine what marketing techniques are acceptable at any given time. Typically, search engines try hard not to flag false-positives as spam, so most algorithms are quite lenient, as long as you do not build lots of low-quality links, host large quantities of duplicate content, or perform other actions that are considered widely outside of relevancy guidelines. If your site is banned from a search engine, you may request reinclusion after fixing the problem.

Spamming

The act of creating and distributing spam.

Spider

Search engine crawlers that search or "spider" the web for pages to include in their index.

Submission

The act of making information systems and related websites aware of your website. In most cases, you no longer need to submit your website to large-scale search engines; they follow links and index content. The best way to submit your site is to get others to link to it.

T

Tagging, Tags (see Bookmarks)

Term Frequency

A measure of how frequently a keyword appears amongst a collection of documents.

Text Link Ads

Advertisements formatted as text links. Since the web was originally based on text and links, people are typically more inclined to pay attention to text links than some other ad formats, which are usually less relevant and more annoying. However, search engines primarily want to count editorial links as votes, so links that are grouped together with other paid links (especially if those links are to off-topic commercial sites) may be less likely to carry weight in search engines.

Title

The title element is used to describe the contents of a document. The title is one of the most important aspects to doing SEO on a web page.

TrustRank

Search relevancy algorithm that places additional weight on links from trusted seed websites controlled by major corporations, educational institutions, or governmental institutions.

U

Unethical SEO

Some search engine marketers lacking in creativity try to market their services as ethical, whereas services rendered by other providers are somehow unethical. SEO services are generally neither ethical nor unethical. They are either effective or ineffective. SEO is an inherently risky business, but any quality SEO service provider should make clients aware of the potential risks and rewards of recommended techniques.

Update

Search engines frequently update their algorithms and data sets to help keep their search results fresh and make their relevancy algorithms hard to duplicate. Most major search engines are continuously updating both their relevancy algorithms and search index.

URL (Uniform Resource Locator)

The unique address of any web document.

Usability

How easy it is for customers to perform the desired actions. The structure and formatting of text and hyperlink-based calls to action can drastically increase your website usability and thus conversion rates.

Usage Data

Things like a large stream of traffic, repeat visitors, multiple page views per visitor, a high click-through rate, or a high level of brand-related search queries may be seen by some search engines as a sign of quality.

V

Vertical Search

A search service focused on a particular field, a particular type of information, or a particular information format.

Viral Marketing

Self-propagating marketing techniques. Common modes of transmission are e-mail, blogging, and word-of-mouth marketing channels. Many social news sites and social bookmarking sites also lead to secondary citations.

Virtual Server

A server that allows multiple top-level domains to be hosted from a single computer. Using a virtual server can save money for smaller applications, but dedicated hosting should be used for large commercial platforms. Most domains are hosted on virtual servers, but using a dedicated server on your most important domains should add server reliability and could be seen as a sign of quality.

W

WHOIS

Each domain has an owner of record. Ownership data is stored in the WHOIS record for that domain. Some domain registrars also allow you to hide the ownership data of your sites. Many large-scale spammers use fake WHOIS data.

White Hat SEO

Search engines set up guidelines that help them extract billions of dollars of ad revenue from the work of publishers and the attention of searchers. Within that highly profitable framework, search engines consider certain marketing techniques deceptive in nature and label them as black hat SEO. Those considered within their guidelines are called white hat SEO techniques. The search guidelines are not a static set of rules, and things that may be considered legitimate one day may be considered deceptive the next.

WordPress

Popular open-source blogging software platform offering both a downloadable blogging program and a hosted solution.

If you are serious about building a brand or making money online, you should publish your content to your own domain because it can be hard to reclaim a website's link equity and age-related trust if you have built years of link equity into a subdomain on someone else's website.

Wordtracker

Feature-rich, paid-keyword research tool that collects data from a couple of popular meta search engines, like Dogpile.

X

XHTML (Extensible Hypertext Markup Language)

A class of specifications designed to move HTML to conform to XML formatting.

XML (Extensible Markup Language)

A simple, very flexible text format derived from SGML, used to make it easy to syndicate or format information using technologies such as RSS.

Y

Yahoo! Site Explorer

Research tool webmasters can use to see which pages Yahoo! has indexed from a website and which pages link at those pages.

YouTube

Feature-rich amateur video upload and syndication website owned by Google.

I want to send out a big thank you to Aaron Wall from SEO Book, **www.seobook.com** *for putting together such an expansive SEO glossary and allowing SEO professionals such as myself to publish this list for others to see.*

About the Author

Matt Davidson is a search marketing expert who has worked in the field of Internet marketing for nearly a decade. Recruited by Microsoft in 2006 to work with advertisers on the company's newly launched paid search platform, adCenter, the author had the unique opportunity to be at the forefront of a major evolution in search engine marketing. During that time, the author also participated in trade marketing for Microsoft, which required spending time on the road attending most of the major search marketing conferences.

After leaving Microsoft, the author went on to launch Sovo Media, an SEO agency. At Sovo Media, he has worked hands-on with companies of all shapes and sizes. The author is passionate about helping small and medium-sized companies devise innovative and inexpensive ways to reach their potential customers. He also presents SEO webinars and works with traditional agencies setting up SEO programs for their clients.

Acknowledgments

First, I would like to thank all of my clients for entrusting their business to me and allowing me to work on their SEO campaigns. Without their trust and feedback, I would never have had the opportunity to experiment with SEO and gain the knowledge needed to put together a book such as this.

I would also like to thank my hardworking team at Sovo Media for all of their great work building our process and for constantly pushing me to improve and learn on a daily basis. I would like to especially thank my business partner, Mike Shin, who has been a tremendous help in ensuring that our work has been able to thrive in a constantly changing and evolving environment.

Thank you to Jason Yormark, who has opened my eyes to the value that social media can play in just about every aspect of online interaction. Your constant encouragement has been a huge motivator to me as my career has continued to evolve in the SEO field.

A special thanks goes out to the folks at Moz who never hesitated to let me share some of the great research they've conducted in the SEO space and who graciously allowed me to present screenshots of their impressive SEO software.

A big thank you is in order for my editor, Susan VanHecke. Without your guidance and keen editorial eye, I have no doubt that this book would have been a disorganized mess that wouldn't have done much good for the greater public.

A big thanks goes out to my family and friends. Without your constant words of encouragement, I would have never been able to maintain the mental stamina and wherewithal to spend those endless days and nights working on this project.

Last but not least, I'd like to thank my better half, Inna Kuperman. I'm not quite sure how you put up with me sometimes, but you seem to manage okay. You've been a huge advocate of mine from day one and have given me the confidence and push needed to make this book happen.

They say it takes a village to raise a child, and in my personal experience, there is definitely some truth to this. Without the inspirational and talented people I find myself surrounded by on a daily basis, this book would have never been possible. So thank you, everyone, for your help in making *Step-by-Step SEO* a reality!

You've Finished the Book. Before You Go...

- **Review us on Amazon**
- **Visit us at www.stepbystepseobook.com**
- **Share on Facebook that you've read this book**
- **Tweet your thoughts on this book**
- **Include this book on your LinkedIn reading list**

I hope you've found this book useful in helping you reach your full potential online.

Made in the USA
Monee, IL
04 November 2026

67378041R00108